CHRONICLES OF COLORADO.

CHRONICLES OF COLORADO

▪FRANCIS PARKMAN ▪ HORACE GREELEY ▪
MARK TWAIN ▪ WALT WHITMAN ▪ ZANE GREY
SAMUEL BOWLES ▪ HELEN HUNT JACKSON ▪
▪EMILY FAITHFULL ▪ RUDYARD KIPLING ▪
ENOS MILLS ▪ THEODORE ROOSEVELT.

Selected and Introduced by
FREDERICK R. RINEHART.

A ROBERTS RINEHART BOOK
TAYLOR TRADE PUBLISHING

Lanham • New York • Oxford

for Alex and C. C.
and in memory of Tom Auer, editor extraordinaire

Taylor Trade
A Roberts Rinehart Book
A wholly owned subsidary of The Rowman & Littlefield Publishing Group, Inc.
4501 Forbes Boulevard, Suite 200
Lanham, MD 20706

Distributed by National Book Network

A previous edition of this book was previously cataloged by the Library of Congress as follows:

Rinehart, Frederick R. (Frederick Roberts), 1953–
    Chronicles of Colorado / selected and introduced by Frederick R. Rinehart.
       p. cm.
    1. Colorado—description and travel. I. Title.
    ISBN 1-58979-045-6 (pbk.: alk. paper)

F776.5 .C5 1984
978.8 19   83062747

Manufactured in the United States of America.

CONTENTS

"Gates of Lodore," northwestern Colorado, as rendered by a nineteenth century engraver.

PREFACE TO THE
THIRD EDITION

When I first put this book together twenty years ago, the population of the state of Colorado was approximately 2.8 million souls. James Michener's novel about the state, *Centennial*, had just been produced as a popular TV miniseries and an oil bust had thrown the local economy into a tailspin, adding credence to the belief that our economy had been historically overly dependent on the fluctuating demand for our vast mineral resources. *Centennial* itself painted a rather gloomy picture of the future by postulating that our limited water supply could barely support our population. It did not hesitate to suggest that any kind of severe drought would bring an immediate halt to residential and commercial development, and unmercifully kill off what was left of our wounded economy.

One catastrophic drought and 1.5 million people later, Colorado has survived and even prospered. Observing the state—especially the people of the state—over twenty years has been an inspiring lesson in the ability of people to adapt creatively to ever changing circumstances. Notwithstanding the 30 percent increase in the state's population, the Front Range corridor managed to shake its reputation as having some of the dirtiest air of any metropolitan area in the United States. A revolution in regional landscape architecture resulted in the development of greenways that take advantage of what nature gives us along cool and shady riparian woodlands. Xeriscaping has become accepted as a worthy alternative to water-intensive gardening and landscaping. Finally, a highly diversified economic base—consisting of high tech, manufacturing, tourism, transportation, services, construction, and finance—has largely subsumed the traditional yet teetering twin pillars of the Colorado economy, agriculture and mining.

Still, the perspective of twenty years allows a little nostalgia for the good old days, when the drive from Boulder to Denver took you by virtually unfettered fields and the jam ups at the Eisenhower Tunnel on Sunday afternoons were the exception rather than the rule. Eastern Colorado now abounds with bedroom communities, golf courses, and elaborate shopping malls, often obscuring, as I suggested in the 1983 introduction to this book, the sublime landscape that drew us here in the first place. I was wrong about one thing in that essay, though: the land is not, as I haughtily proclaimed, "intolerant of the excesses of human habitation." For one thing, tolerance is a human characteristic; for another, although there are more of us, we have significantly curbed our individual excesses. One of the ironies of moving from supposedly idyllic, rural Colorado to a "planned community" of several hundred homes, as I have in recent years, is that new construction is marvelously efficient in its energy consumption and water use. I now cringe at how we used to "flood irrigate" our pastures and tolerate smoke-belching farm equipment that was subject to no emissions laws.

*   *   *

More vexing for me over the past two decades has been what I will call (for lack of a better expression) "a search for identity." This is not so much a question of whether or not Colorado is a good place to live (it is), but more an exploration of what makes us uniquely Coloradan— and what makes Colorado unique. Certainly being the "highest state" is a cachet that leaves you with the impression that we are the head and shoulders of the continent, looking down our ski-sloped nose on the "flattest state" or the "lowest state." Perhaps one in four Coloradans knows that we are also the Centennial State, owing to our entry into the Union in 1876. Neither moniker, however, alludes to any great cultural tradition that bonds us irrevocably to this land (though I still contend that Colorado geography has shaped us more than we have shaped it). Wyoming is clearly the Cowboy State. Utah has its Mormon traditions. New Mexico prides itself on its Hispanic and Native American heritages. Colorado has ski resorts, a substantial urban strip from Fort Collins to Pueblo, and a really big airport. Indeed, so transient is the social environment of Colorado that our state motto could easily be "just passing through."

In rereading the selections in this volume recently, I became aware of how the state seems to redefine itself about once a generation, not terribly surprising for a place with so much mobility—upward, downward, outward, inward. To Francis Parkman (1846) it was an unfriendly place that one hurried to get through. Thirteen years later the discovery of gold and silver moved Horace Greeley to observe, "All is now being rapidly changed, and not entirely for the better." By 1879 Colorado had within it a strong urban presence, with Walt Whitman marveling over the salubrious atmosphere of Denver: "there has steadily grown upon me a feeling of affection for the spot." In the early twentieth century, with civilization well established on the eastern plains and a ski industry still years from development, Zane Grey, Theodore Roosevelt, and Enos Mills shifted the focus to the Colorado wilderness, a golden era for the outdoorsman if there ever was one.

Since I'm at the age where we start talking about such things, the topic of what to do after the kids have flown the coop now frequently comes up in conversations with friends. Although I have no statistical data to back this up, my sense is that more than half plan to leave the state either upon or near retirement. Some are going "back to" . . . fill in the blanks: New England, Seattle, Charleston. Some plan to make the inevitable migration to a warmer climate. Others want to live by the sea. Immigrants ourselves, my wife and I haven't yet decided just what we're going to do. We could just as happily live out our lives in Colorado as move on. Curiously, though, I am insistent upon one thing: that upon our demise, our ashes are to be interred in the family plot in Dutchess County, New York, where my ancestors were first laid to rest 200 years before Colorado became a state.

Just passing through, I suppose.

Frederick R. Rinehart
Boulder, January 2003

INTRODUCTION

The understanding of history can be a strain on the imagination. How can one conceive of the harsh crossing of the Colorado prairie by our forebears when that same prairie is now conveniently criss-crossed with interstates and dotted with fast-food stores? How do we visualize a buffalo herd that extends to the horizon, a drouth that means something more than brown lawns, or imagine the Colorado River running undammed from its headwaters to the Gulf of California?

The problem does not lend itself to an easy solution. As a child, visiting the historic sites of the East, I was often put off by the presence of some modern-day convenience—an anachronism, if you will—standing next to an artifact of our history. Visually, the presence of parked cars by historic sites such as Williamsburg or Bent's Fort is an uneasy compromise between our fascination with history and our desire to make the past accessible. The imagination extends and tries to block out what shouldn't be there, but the net effect is that the whole thing has been put up, like Main Street at Disneyland.

Historians in their best prose have not done much better. They work at a distinct disadvantage, for their knowledge of the lands and peoples about which they write is usually second-hand. This disadvantage is probably compounded in writing about Colorado, for no superlative seems adequate to describe the state's remarkable geography: it must be seen to be believed. To the extent that the state's geography might tell us something about the history of Colorado, it is only helpful in showing where civilization has passed: the continuity of a green forest is broken here and there by brown blemishes of century-old tailings piles; old stone walls leap out of improbable places, like Carthage grown over. The imagination is left to do a great deal of work, creating interpretative problems for practicing historians and limitless wondering for the rest of us.

It is for these reasons that this collection of first-hand accounts of

Colorado over a period of seventy-four years has been assembled. These essays show Colorado at various intervals in its early history; in effect, they are "eyewitness accounts" subject to the writer's interpretation of what he or she saw.

I have rather arbitrarily determined that the writings included here should begin with an account by perhaps the first truly prominent writer to say something about Colorado, Francis Parkman, and end with a tale by Enos Mills written about the time the collective memories of our parents and grandparents fail us. In almost all cases the authors of these accounts will be known to readers; this was intentional. And without exception their impressions of the state were written for a national, and in a few cases international, audience. Two of the writers whose essays I have included here, Helen Hunt Jackson and Enos Mills, were Colorado residents, but their publishers were in the East and both writers were known to readers throughout the English-speaking world. Except for these two writers, I have emphasized impressions of early Colorado from the vantage point of the outsider.

The selections are arranged chronologically and with an eye toward the geographic diversity of the state. Along the way I have tried to present historical information to provide background for the chronicles and their authors, but with a minimum of scholarly apparatus. For while acknowledging the historical utility of a book of readings such as this one, another of my intentions has been to assemble a book that will make for pleasant reading whether on the trail, in the classroom, or in the easy chair. From the free-flowing prose of Walt Whitman to the riotous accounts of Mark Twain and Rudyard Kipling, to the adventure tales of Enos Mills, Theodore Roosevelt, and Zane Grey, a portrait of early Colorado emerges in a literary tapestry as diverse as the state's history.

Yet even in a book presenting many different perspectives on the progress of a society, a consistent theme can be discerned: the important role that the land itself has played in shaping the character of Coloradans from the first white settlers of the 1850s to the present citizens. It is to the land itself and not the philosophic musings of utopianists or city planners that Coloradans have looked for their wealth, recreation, and spiritual fulfillment. The land, more than the spirit of rugged individualism (largely invented in fiction), has been the true heritage of the West; the land itself is what modern Coloradans share with their forebears.

Unfortunately, however, the wonder of the Colorado landscape is an experience exclusive to no one. And for all its popularity over the years, it is a land intolerant of the excesses of human habitation. Although Horace Greeley described in 1859 a Colorado whose "air is singularly pure and bracing," whose "solitude was sylvan and perfect," by 1883 the tide of settlement had prompted Helen Hunt Jackson to complain of huge mounds of tin cans at abandoned mining camps and polluted water running down from active camps. In our own day the unpleasant vestiges of these and other settlements remind us that development of the land implies the responsibility to restore it for future generations.

But if certain areas of the West—where shopping centers, steel mills, and highways rival buttes, ravines, and cottonwood groves for a place on the landscape—tax one's historical imagination of the early days, then still others "bankrupt it," as Theodore Roosevelt once claimed. In spite of relatively high population density, the ear-numbing presence of jeeps and dirt-bikes on our wilderness trails, and a ubiquitous resort industry, the land has prevailed, providing native Coloradans and visitors alike a rejuvenation best described by Zane Grey in his later years:

> To feel the wind in your face; to ride in the teeth of a sandstorm and flying dust and furious squall; to feel the cold of dawn nip your ears and the heat of noon burn your back; to hear the thunder of the Colorado and the roar of mountain streams, and the rustle of sand through the sage, and the moan of the night breeze in the spruce, the mourn of the wolf and the whistle of the stag; to feel the silence and loneliness of the desert—all this is to grow young again.[1]

FRANCIS PARKMAN.

1846

It is difficult for the contemporary Coloradan to believe that his backyard was once perceived as "an arid desert . . . [whose] only vegetation was a few tufts of short grass, dried and shrivelled by the heat."[2] But widespread use of irrigation over the years has given this region the veil of Eden, so many of us forget that this land was at one time considered uninhabitable. Indeed, travellers to eastern Colorado* in the early nineteenth century were most anxious to get any journey across the plains over with as soon as possible.

Of these early visitors to Colorado, Francis Parkman was among the most literate and perceptive. The young Boston Brahmin travelled west with his cousin Quincy Adams Shaw in 1846, supposedly to seek a cure for his mysterious fits of blindness, but more likely to satisfy his curiosity about the West and the Red Man. His classic account of the expedition is *The Oregon Trail,* a book which made Parkman the most widely read historian of his time. In a chapter appropriately titled "The Lonely Journey" Parkman recounts what it was like to travel south across the hostile Colorado prairie on the way from Fort Laramie, Wyoming to a town that was to become Pueblo, Colorado.

---

*These travellers of course hadn't the slightest idea that they were in a place called Colorado—in fact, much of Colorado in 1846 still belonged to Mexico, and Colorado was not so named until it became a recognized territory of the United States in 1861.

THE
LONELY
JOURNEY

ON THE DAY OF MY AR-
rival at Fort Laramie, Shaw and I were lounging on two buffalo-robes
in the large apartment hospitably assigned to us; Henry Chatillon also
was present, busy about the harness and weapons, which had been
brought into the room, and two or three Indians were crouching on
the floor, eying us with their fixed, unwavering gaze.

"I have been well off here," said Shaw, "in all respects but one; there
is no good *shongsasha* to be had for love or money."

I gave him a small leather bag containing some of excellent quality,
which I had brought from the Black Hills. "Now, Henry," said he, "hand
me Papin's chopping-board, or give it to that Indian, and let him cut
the mixture; they understand it better than any white man."

The Indian, without saying a word, mixed the bark and the tobacco
in due proportions, filled the pipe, and lighted it. This done, my companion and I proceeded to deliberate on our future course of proceed-
ing; first, however, Shaw acquainted me with some incidents which
had occurred at the fort during my absence.

About a week before, four men had arrived from beyond the mountains: Sublette, Reddick, and two others. Just before reaching the fort,
they had met a large party of Indians, chiefly young men. All of them
belonged to the village of our old friend Smoke, who, with his whole
band of adherents, professed the greatest friendship for the whites. The
travellers therefore approached and began to converse without the least
suspicion. Suddenly, however, their bridles were seized, and they were
ordered to dismount. Instead of complying, they lashed their horses,

4

and broke away from the Indians. As they galloped off, they heard a yell behind them, with a burst of derisive laughter, and the reports of several guns. None of them were hurt, though Reddick's bridle-rein was cut by a bullet within an inch of his hand. After this taste of Indian manners, they felt for the moment no disposition to encounter farther risks. They intended to pursue the route southward along the foot of the mountains to Bent's Fort; and as our plans coincided with theirs, they proposed to join forces. Finding, however, that I did not return, they grew impatient of inaction, forgot their late danger, and set out without us, promising to wait our arrival at Bent's Fort. From thence we were to make the long journey to the settlements in company, as the path was not a little dangerous, being infested by hostile Pawnees and Camanches.

We expected, on reaching Bent's Fort, to find there still another reinforcement. A young Kentuckian had come out to the mountains with Russel's party of California emigrants. One of his chief objects, as he gave out, was to kill an Indian; an exploit which he afterwards succeeded in achieving, much to the jeopardy of ourselves, and others who had to pass through the country of the dead Pawnee's enraged relatives. Having become disgusted with his emigrant associates, he left them, and had some time before set out with a party of companions for the head of the Arkansas. He left us a letter, to say that he would wait until we arrived at Bent's Fort, and accompany us thence to the settlements. When, however, he came to the fort, he found there a party of forty men about to make the homeward journey, and wisely preferred to avail himself of so strong an escort. Sublette and his companions also joined this company; so that on reaching Bent's Fort, some six weeks after, we found ourselves deserted by our allies and thrown once more upon our own resources.

On the fourth of August, early in the afternoon, we bade a final adieu to the hospitable gateway of Fort Laramie. Again Shaw and I were riding side by side on the prairie. For the first fifty miles we had companions with us: Troché, a trapper, and Rouville, a nondescript in the employ of the Fur Company, who were going to join the trader Bisonette at his encampment near the head of Horse Creek. We rode only six or eight miles that afternoon before we came to a little brook traversing the barren prairie. All along its course grew copses of young wild-cherry trees, loaded with ripe fruit, and almost concealing the gliding thread of water with their dense growth. Here we encamped;

and being too indolent to pitch our tent, we flung our saddles on the ground, spread a pair of buffalo-robes, lay down upon them, and began to smoke. Meanwhile Deslauriers busied himself with his frying-pan, and Raymond stood guard over the band of grazing horses. Deslauriers had an active assistant in Rouville, who professed great skill in the culinary art, and, seizing upon a fork, began to lend his aid in cooking supper. Indeed, according to his own belief, Rouville was a man of universal knowledge, and he lost no opportunity to display his manifold accomplishments. He had been a circus-rider at St. Louis, and once he rode round Fort Laramie on his head, to the utter bewilderment of the Indians. He was also noted as the wit of the fort; and as he had considerable humor and abundant vivacity, he contributed more that night to the liveliness of the camp than all the rest of the party put together. At one instant he would kneel by Deslauriers, instructing him in the true method of frying antelope-steaks, then he would come and seat himself at our side, dilating upon the correct fashion of braiding up a horse's tail, telling apocryphal stories how he had killed a buffalo bull with a knife, having first cut off his tail when at full speed, or relating whimsical anecdotes of the *bourgeois* Papin. At last he snatched up a volume of Shakespeare that was lying on the grass, and halted and stumbled through a line or two to prove that he could read. He went gambolling about the camp, chattering like some frolicsome ape; and whatever he was doing at one moment, the presumption was a sure one that he would not be doing it the next. His companion Troché sat silently on the grass, not speaking a word, but keeping a vigilant eye on a very ugly little Utah squaw, of whom he was extremely jealous.

On the next day we travelled farther, crossing the wide sterile basin called "Goché's Hole." Towards night we became involved among ravines; and being unable to find water, our journey was protracted to a very late hour. On the next morning we had to pass a long line of bluffs, whose raw sides, wrought upon by rains and storms, were of a ghastly whiteness most oppressive to the sight. As we ascended a gap in these hills, the way was marked by huge footprints, like those of a human giant. They were the tracks of the grizzly bear, of which we had also seen abundance on the day before. Immediately after this we were crossing a barren plain, spreading in long and gentle undulations to the horizon. Though the sun was bright, there was a light haze in the atmosphere. The distant hills assumed strange, distorted forms in the mirage, and the edge of the horizon was continually changing

"Again Shaw and I were riding side by side on the prairie." Illustration by Frederic Remington.

its aspect. Shaw and I were riding together, and Henry Chatillon was a few rods before us, when he stopped his horse suddenly, and turning round with the peculiar earnest expression which he always wore when excited, called us to come forward. We galloped to his side. Henry pointed towards a black speck on the gray swell of the prairie, apparently about a mile off. "It must be a bear," said he; "come, now we shall all have some sport. Better fun to fight him than to fight an old buffalo bull; grizzly bear so strong and smart."

So we all galloped forward together, prepared for a hard fight; for these bears, though clumsy in appearance, are incredibly fierce and active. The swell of the prairie concealed the black object from our view. Immediately after it appeared again. But now it seemed very near to us; and as we looked at it in astonishment, it suddenly separated into two parts, each of which took wing and flew away. We stopped our horses and looked at Henry, whose face exhibited a curious mixture of mirth and mortification. His eye had been so completely deceived by the peculiar atmosphere that he had mistaken two large crows at the distance of fifty rods for a grizzly bear a mile off. To the journey's end Henry never heard the last of the grizzly bear with wings.

In the afternoon we came to the foot of a considerable hill. As we ascended it, Rouville began to ask questions concerning our condition and prospects at home, and Shaw was edifying him with an account of an imaginary wife and child, to which he listened with implicit faith. Reaching the top of the hill, we saw the windings of Horse Creek on the plains below us, and a little on the left we could distinguish the camp of Bisonette among the trees and copses along the course of the stream. Rouville's face assumed just then a ludicrously blank expression. We inquired what was the matter; when it appeared that Bisonette had sent him from this place to Fort Laramie with the sole object of bringing back a supply of tobacco. Our rattlebrain friend, from the time of his reaching the fort up to the present moment, had entirely forgotten the object of his journey, and had ridden a dangerous hundred miles for nothing. Descending to Horse Creek, we forded it, and on the opposite bank a solitary Indian sat on horseback under a tree. He said nothing, but turned and led the way towards the camp. Bisonette had made choice of an admirable position. The stream, with its thick growth of trees, enclosed on three sides a wide green meadow, where about forty Dahcotah lodges were pitched in a circle, and beyond them a few lodges of the friendly Shiennes. Bisonette himself lived in the Indian manner. Riding up to his lodge, we found him seated at the head of it, surrounded by various appliances of comfort not common on the prairie. His squaw was near him, and rosy children were scrambling about in printed calico gowns; Paul Dorion, also, with his leathery face and old white capote, was seated in the lodge, together with Antoine Le Rouge, a half-breed Pawnee, Sibille, a trader, and several other white men.

"It will do you no harm," said Bisonette, "to stay here with us for a day or two, before you start for the Pueblo."

We accepted the invitation, and pitched our tent on a rising ground above the camp and close to the trees. Bisonette soon invited us to a feast, and we suffered abundance of the same sort of attention from his Indian associates. The reader may possibly recollect that when I joined the Indian village, beyond the Black Hills, I found that a few families were absent, having declined to pass the mountains along with the rest. The Indians in Bisonette's camp consisted of these very families, and many of them came to me that evening to inquire after their relatives and friends. They were not a little mortified to learn that while they, from their own timidity and indolence, were almost in a starving condition, the rest of the village had provided their lodges for the next season, laid in a great stock of provisions, and were living in abundance. Bisonette's companions had been sustaining themselves for some time on wild cherries, which the squaws pounded, stones and all, and spread on buffalo-robes to dry in the sun; they were then eaten without farther preparation, or used as an ingredient in various delectable compounds.

On the next day, the camp was in commotion with a new arrival. A single Indian had come with his family from the Arkansas. As he passed among the lodges, he put on an expression of unusual dignity and importance, and gave out that he had brought great news to tell the whites. Soon after the squaws had pitched his lodge, he sent his little son to invite all the white men and all the more distinguished Indians to a feast. The guests arrived and sat wedged together, shoulder to shoulder, within the hot and suffocating lodge. The Stabber, for that was our entertainer's name, had killed an old buffalo bull on his way. This veteran's boiled tripe, tougher than leather, formed the main item of the repast. For the rest, it consisted of wild cherries and grease boiled together in a large copper kettle. The feast was distributed, and for a moment all was silent, strenuous exertion; then each guest, though with one or two exceptions, turned his wooden dish bottom upwards to prove that he had done full justice to his entertainer's hospitality. The Stabber next produced his chopping-board, on which he prepared the mixture for smoking, and filled several pipes, which circulated among the company. This done, he seated himself upright on his couch, and began with much gesticulation to tell his story. I will not repeat his childish jargon. It was so entangled, like the greater part of an Indian's stories, with absurd and contradictory details, that it was almost impossible to disengage from it a single particle of truth. All that we could gather was the following:—

He had been on the Arkansas, and there he had seen six great war-parties of whites. He had never believed before that the whole world contained half so many white men. They all had large horses, long knives, and short rifles, and some of them were dressed alike in the most splendid war-dresses he had ever seen. From this account it was clear that bodies of dragoons and perhaps also of volunteer cavalry had passed up the Arkansas. The Stabber had also seen a great many of the white lodges of the Meneaska, drawn by their long-horned buffalo. These could be nothing else than covered ox-wagons, used, no doubt, in transporting stores for the troops. Soon after seeing this, our host had met an Indian who had lately come from among the Camanches, who had told him that all the Mexicans had gone out to a great buffalo hunt; that the Americans had hid themselves in a ravine; and that when the Mexicans had shot away all their arrows, the Americans fired their guns, raised their war-whoop, rushed out, and killed them all. We could only infer from this, that war had been declared with Mexico, and a battle fought in which the Americans were victorious. When, some weeks after, we arrived at the Pueblo, we heard of General Kearney's march up the Arkansas, and of General Taylor's victories at Matamoras.

As the sun was setting that evening a crowd gathered on the plain by the side of our tent, to try the speed of their horses. These were of every shape, size, and color. Some came from California, some from the States, some from among the mountains, and some from the wild bands of the prairie. They were of every hue, white, black, red, and gray, or mottled and clouded with a strange variety of colors. They all had a wild and startled look, very different from the sober aspect of a well-bred city steed. Those most noted for swiftness and spirit were decorated with eagle feathers dangling from their manes and tails. Fifty or sixty Dahcotah were present, wrapped from head to foot in their heavy robes of whitened hide. There were also a considerable number of the Shiennes, many of whom wore gaudy Mexican ponchos, swathed around their shoulders, but leaving the right arm bare. Mingled among the crowd of Indians was a number of Canadians, chiefly in the employ of Bisonette,—men whose home is the wilderness, and who love the campfire better than the domestic hearth. They are contented and happy in the midst of hardship, privation, and danger. Their cheerfulness and gayety is irrepressible, and no people on earth understand better how "to daff the world aside and bid it pass." Besides these, were two or three half-breeds, a race of rather extraordinary composition, being according to the common saying half Indian, half white man, and half devil. Antoine Le Rouge was the most conspicuous among them, with his loose trousers and fluttering calico shirt. A handkerchief was bound round his head to confine his black snaky hair, and his small eyes twinkled beneath it with a mischievous lustre. He had a fine cream-colored horse, whose speed he must needs try along with the rest. So he threw off the rude high-peaked saddle, and substituting a piece of buffalo-robe, leaped lightly into his seat. The space was cleared, the word was given, and he and his Indian rival darted out like lightning from among the crowd, each stretching forward over his horse's neck and plying his heavy Indian whip with might and main. A moment, and both were lost in the gloom; but Antoine soon came riding back victorious, exultingly patting the neck of his quivering and panting horse.

About midnight, as I lay asleep, wrapped in a buffalo-robe on the ground by the side of our cart, Raymond came and woke me. Something, he said, was going forward which I would like to see. Looking down into the camp, I saw on the farther side of it a great number of Indians gathered about a fire, the bright glare of which made them visible through the thick darkness; while from the midst proceeded a loud, measured chant which would have killed Paganini outright, broken occasionally by a burst of sharp yells. I gathered the robe around me, for the night was cold, and walked down to the spot. The dark throng of Indians was so dense that they almost intercepted the light of the flame. As I was pushing among them with little ceremony, a chief interposed himself, and I was given to understand that a white man must not approach the scene of their solemnities too closely. By passing round to the other side where there was a little opening in the crowd, I could see clearly what was going forward, without intruding my unhallowed presence into the inner circle. The society of the "Strong Hearts" were engaged in one of their dances. The "Strong Hearts" are a warlike association, comprising men of both the Dahcotah and Shienne nations, and entirely composed, or supposed to be so, of young braves of the highest mettle. Its fundamental principle is the admirable one of never retreating from any enterprise once begun. All these Indian associations have a tutelary spirit. That of the Strong Hearts is embodied in the fox, an animal which white men would hardly have selected for a similar purpose, though his subtle character agrees well enough with an Indian's notions of what is honorable in warfare. The dancers were circling round and round the fire, each figure brightly illumined at one moment by the yellow light, and at the next drawn in blackest shadow as it passed between the flame and the spectator. They would imitate with the most ludicrous exactness the motions and voice of their sly patron the fox. Then a startling yell would be given. Many other warriors would leap into the ring, and with faces upturned towards the starless sky, they would all stamp, and whoop, and brandish their weapons like so many frantic devils.

We remained here till the next afternoon. My companion and I with our three attendants then set out for the Pueblo, a distance of three hundred miles, and we supposed the journey would occupy about a fortnight. During this time we all hoped that we might not meet a single human being, for should we encounter any, they would in all probability be enemies, in whose eyes our rifles would be our only passports. For the first two days nothing worth mentioning took place. On the third morning, however, an untoward incident occurred. We were encamped by the side of a little brook in an extensive hollow of the plain. Deslauriers was up long before daylight, and before he began to prepare breakfast he turned loose all the horses, as in duty bound. There was a cold mist clinging close to the ground, and by the time the rest of us were awake the animals were invisible. It was only after a long and anxious search that we could discover by their tracks the direction they had taken. They had all set off for Fort Laramie, following the guidance of a mutinous old mule, and though many of them were hobbled, they travelled three miles before they could be overtaken and driven back.

For two or three days, we were passing over an arid desert. The only vegetation was a few tufts of short grass, dried and shrivelled by the heat. There was an abundance of strange insects and reptiles. Huge crickets, black and bottle green, and wingless grasshoppers of the most extravagant dimensions, were tumbling about our horses' feet, and lizards without number darting like lightning among the tufts of grass. The most curious animal, however, was that commonly called the horned-frog. I caught one of them and consigned him to the care of Deslauriers, who tied him up in a moccason. About a month after this, I examined the prisoner's condition, and finding him still lively and active, I provided him with a cage of buffalo-hide, which was hung up in the cart. In this manner he arrived safely at the settlements. From thence he travelled the whole way to Boston, packed closely in a trunk, being regaled with fresh air regularly every night. When he reached his destination he was deposited under a glass case, where he sat for some months in great tranquillity, alternately dilating and contracting his white throat to the admiration of his visitors. At length, one morning about the middle of winter, he gave up the ghost, and he now occupies a bottle of alcohol in the Agassiz Museum. His death was attributed to starvation, a very probable conclusion, since for six months he had taken no food whatever, though the sympathy of his juvenile admirers had tempted his palate with a great variety of delicacies. We found also animals of a somewhat larger growth. The number of prairie-dogs was astounding. Frequently the hard and dry plain was thickly covered, for miles together, with the little mounds which they make at the mouth of their burrows, and small squeaking voices yelped at us, as we passed along. The noses of the inhabitants were just visible at the mouth of their holes, but no sooner was their curiosity satisfied than they would instantly vanish. Some of the bolder dogs—though in fact they are no dogs at all, but little marmots rather smaller than a rabbit—would sit yelping at us on the top of their mounds, jerking their tails emphatically with every shrill cry they uttered. As the danger drew nearer they would wheel about, toss their heels into the air, and dive in a twinkling into their burrows. Towards sunset, and especially if rain was threatening, the whole community made their appearance above ground. We saw them gathered in large knots around the burrow of some favorite citizen. There they would all sit erect, their tails spread out on the ground, and their paws hanging down before their white breasts, chattering and squeaking with the utmost vivacity upon some topic of common interest, while the proprietor of the burrow sat on the top of his mound, looking down with a complacent countenance on the enjoyment of his guests. Meanwhile, others ran about from burrow to burrow, as if on some errand of the last importance to their subterranean commonwealth. The snakes are apparently the prairie-dog's worst enemies; at least I think too well of the latter to suppose that they associate on friendly terms with these slimy intruders, which may be seen at all times basking among their holes, into which they always retreat when disturbed. Small owls, with wise and grave countenances, also make their abode with the prairie-dogs, though on what terms they live together I could never ascertain.

On the fifth day after leaving Bisonette's camp, we saw, late in the afternoon, what we supposed to be a considerable stream, but on approaching it, we found to our mortification nothing but a dry bed of sand, into which the water had sunk and disappeared. We separated, some riding in one direction and some in another, along its course. Still we found no traces of water, not even so much as a wet spot in the sand. The old cotton-wood trees that grew along the bank, lamentably abused by lightning and tempest, were withering with the drought, and on the dead limbs, at the summit of the tallest, half a dozen crows were hoarsely cawing, like birds of evil omen. We had no alternative but to keep on. There was no water nearer than the South Fork of the Platte, about ten miles distant. We moved forward, angry and silent, over a desert as flat as the outspread ocean.

The sky had been obscured since the morning by thin mists and vapors, but now vast piles of clouds were gathered together in the west. They rose to a great height above the horizon, and looking up at them I distinguished one mass darker than the rest, and of a peculiar conical form. I happened to look again, and still could see it as before. At some moments it was dimly visible, at others its outline was sharp and distinct; but while the clouds around it were shifting, changing, and dissolving away, it still towered aloft in the midst of them, fixed and immovable. It must, thought I, be the summit of a mountain; and yet its height staggered me. My conclusion was right, however. It was Long's Peak, once believed to be one of the highest of the Rocky Mountain chain, though more recent discoveries have proved the contrary. The thickening gloom soon hid it from view, and we never saw it again, for on the following day, and for some time after, the air was so full of mist that the view of distant objects was entirely cut off.

It grew very late. Turning from our direct course, we made for the river at its nearest point, though in the utter darkness it was not easy to direct our way with much precision. Raymond rode on one side and Henry on the other. We heard each of them shouting that he had come upon a deep ravine. We steered at random between Scylla and Charybdis, and soon after became, as it seemed, inextricably involved with deep chasms all around us, while the darkness was such that we could not see a rod in any direction. We partially extricated ourselves by scrambling, cart and all, through a shallow ravine. We came next to a steep descent, down which we plunged without well knowing what was at the bottom. There was a great cracking of sticks and dry twigs. Over our heads were certain large shadowy objects; and in front something like the faint gleaming of a dark sheet of water. Raymond ran his horse against a tree; Henry alighted, and, feeling on the ground, declared that there was grass enough for the horses. Before taking off his saddle, each man led his own horses down to the water in the best way he could. Then picketing two or three of the evil-disposed, we turned the rest loose, and lay down among the dry sticks to sleep. In the morning we found ourselves close to the South Fork of the Platte, on a spot surrounded by bushes and rank grass. Compensating ourselves with a hearty breakfast for the ill-fare of the previous night, we set forward again on our journey. When only two or three rods from the camp, I saw Shaw stop his mule, level his gun, and fire at some object in the grass. Deslauriers next jumped forward, and began to dance about, belaboring the unseen enemy with a whip. Then he stooped down, and drew out of the grass by the neck an enormous rattlesnake, with his head completely shattered by Shaw's bullet. As Deslauriers held him out at arm's length with an exulting grin, his tail, which still kept slowly writhing about, almost touched the ground; and his body in the largest part was as thick as a stout man's arm. He had fourteen rattles, but the end of his tail was blunted, as if he could once have boasted of many more. From this time till we reached the Pueblo, we killed at least four or five of these snakes every day, as they lay coiled and rattling on the hot sand. Shaw was the St. Patrick of the party, and whenever he killed a snake he pulled off his tail and stored it away in his bullet-pouch, which was soon crammed with an edifying collection of rattles, great and small. Deslauriers with his whip also came in for a share of praise. A day or two after this, he triumphantly produced a small snake about a span and a half long, with one infant rattle at the end of his tail.

We forded the South Fork of the Platte. On its farther bank were the traces of a very large camp of Arapahoes. The ashes of some three hundred fires were visible among the scattered trees, together with the remains of sweating lodges, and all the other appurtenances of a permanent camp. The place, however, had been for some months deserted. A few miles farther on we found more recent signs of Indians; the trail of two or three lodges, which had evidently passed the day before; every footprint was perfectly distinct in the dry, dusty soil. We noticed in particular the track of one moccason, upon the sole of which its economical proprietor had placed a large patch. These signs gave us but little uneasiness, as the number of the warriors scarcely exceeded that of our own party. At noon we rested under the walls of a large fort, built in these solitudes some years since by M. St. Vrain. It was now abandoned and fast falling into ruin. The walls of unbaked bricks were cracked from top to bottom. Our horses recoiled in terror from the neglected entrance, where the heavy gates were torn from their hinges and flung down. The area within was overgrown with weeds, and the long ranges of apartments once occupied by the motley concourse of traders, Canadians, and squaws, were now miserably dilapidated. Twelve miles farther on, near the spot where we encamped, were the remains of another fort, standing in melancholy desertion and neglect.

Early on the following morning we made a startling discovery. We passed close by a large deserted encampment of Arapahoes. There were about fifty fires still smouldering on the ground, and it was evident from numerous signs that the Indians must have left the place within two hours of our reaching it. Their trail crossed our own, at right angles, and led in the direction of a line of hills, half a mile on our left. There were women and children in the party, which would have greatly diminished the danger of encountering them. Henry Chatillon examined the encampment and the trail with a very professional and business-like air.

"Supposing we had met them, Henry?" said I.

The Front Range near Denver as Francis Parkman may have seen it.

"Why," said he, "we hold out our hands to them, and give them all we've got; they take away everything, and then I believe they no kill us. Perhaps," added he, looking up with a quiet, unchanged face, "perhaps we no let them rob us. Maybe before they come near, we have a chance to get into a ravine, or under the bank of the river; then, you know, we fight them."

About noon on that day we reached Cherry Creek.* Here was a great abundance of wild cherries, plums, gooseberries, and currants. The stream, however, like most of the others which we passed, was dried up with the heat, and we had to dig holes in the sand to find water for ourselves and our horses. Two days after, we left the banks of the creek, which we had been following for some time, and began to cross the high dividing ridge which separates the waters of the Platte from those of the Arkansas. The scenery was altogether changed. In place of the burning plains, we passed through rough and savage glens, and among hills crowned with a dreary growth of pines. We encamped among these solitudes on the night of the sixteenth of August. A tempest was threatening. The sun went down among volumes of jet-black cloud, edged with a bloody red. But in spite of these portentous signs, we neglected to put up the tent, and being extremely fatigued, lay down on the ground and fell asleep. The storm broke about midnight, and we pitched the tent amid darkness and confusion. In the morning all was fair again, and Pike's Peak, white with snow, was towering above the wilderness far off.

We pushed through an extensive tract of pine woods. Large black-squirrels were leaping among the branches. From the farther edge of this forest we saw the prairie again, hollowed out before us into a vast basin, and about a mile in front we could discern a little black speck moving upon its surface. It could be nothing but a buffalo. Henry primed his rifle afresh and galloped forward. To the left of the animal was a low rocky mound, of which Henry availed himself in making his approach. After a short time we heard the faint report of the rifle. The bull, mortally wounded from a distance of nearly three hundred yards, ran wildly round and round in a circle. Shaw and I then galloped forward, and passing him as he ran, foaming with rage and pain, discharged our pistols into his side. Once or twice he rushed furiously upon us, but his strength was rapidly exhausted. Down he fell on his knees. For

---

*The present location of Denver.

one instant he glared up at his enemies, with burning eyes, through his black tangled mane, and then rolled over on his side. Though gaunt and thin, he was larger and heavier than the largest ox. Foam and blood flowed together from his nostrils as he lay bellowing and pawing the ground, tearing up grass and earth with his hoofs. His sides rose and fell like a vast pair of bellows, the blood spouting up in jets from the bullet-holes. Suddenly his glaring eyes became like a lifeless jelly. He lay motionless on the ground. Henry stooped over him, and, making an incision with his knife, pronounced the meat too rank and tough for use; so, disappointed in our hopes of an addition to our stock of provisions, we rode away and left the carcass to the wolves.

In the afternoon we saw the mountains rising like a gigantic wall at no great distance on our right. *"Des sauvages! des sauvages!"* exclaimed Deslauriers, looking round with a frightened face, and pointing with his whip towards the foot of the mountains. In fact, we could see at a distance a number of little black specks, like horsemen in rapid motion. Henry Chatillon, with Shaw and myself, galloped towards them to reconnoitre, when to our amusement we saw the supposed Arapahoes resolved into the black tops of some pine-trees which grew along a ravine. The summits of these pines, just visible above the verge of the prairie, and seeming to move as we ourselves were advancing, looked exactly like a line of horsemen.

We encamped among ravines and hollows, through which a little brook was foaming angrily. Before sunrise in the morning the snow-covered mountains were beautifully tinged with a delicate rose-color. A noble spectacle awaited us as we moved forward. Six or eight miles on our right, Pike's Peak and his giant brethren rose out of the level prairie, as if springing from the bed of the ocean. From their summits down to the plain below they were involved in a mantle of clouds, in restless motion, as if urged by strong winds. For one instant some snowy peak, towering in awful solitude, would be disclosed to view. As the clouds broke along the mountain, we could see the dreary forests, the tremendous precipices, the white patches of snow, the gulfs and chasms as black as night, all revealed for an instant, and then disappearing from the view.

On the day after, we had left the mountains at some distance. A black cloud descended upon them, and a tremendous explosion of thunder followed, reverberating among the precipices. In a few moments everything grew black, and the rain poured down like a cataract. We got under an old cotton-wood tree, which stood by the side of a stream, and waited there till the rage of the torrent had passed.

The clouds opened at the point where they first had gathered, and the whole sublime congregation of mountains was bathed at once in warm sunshine. They seemed more like some vision of eastern romance than like a reality of that wilderness; all were melted together into a soft delicious blue, as voluptuous as the sky of Naples or the transparent sea that washes the sunny cliffs of Capri. On the left the sky was still of an inky blackness; but two concentric rainbows stood in bright relief against it, while far in front the ragged clouds still streamed before the wind, and the retreating thunder muttered angrily.

Through that afternoon and the next morning we were passing down the banks of the stream, called "Boiling Spring Creek," from the boiling spring whose waters flow into it. When we stopped at noon, we were within six or eight miles of the Pueblo. Setting out again, we found by the fresh tracks that a horseman had just been out to reconnoitre us; he had circled half round the camp, and then galloped back at full speed for the Pueblo. What made him so shy of us we could not conceive. After an hour's ride we reached the edge of a hill, from which a welcome sight greeted us. The Arkansas ran along the valley below, among woods and groves, and closely nestled in the midst of wide corn-fields and green meadows, where cattle were grazing, rose the low mud walls of the Pueblo.

HORACE GREELEY.

1859

It is unfortunate that Horace Greeley is best remembered today for an adage ("Go west, young man") which in all likelihood has been falsely attributed to him. In addition to being a well-known advocate of western expansion, Greeley was also founder of the New York *Tribune*, U.S. Representative to Congress for one term, participant in the founding of the Republican Party, delegate to the Republican National Convention that nominated Abraham Lincoln for president in 1860, and finally, unsuccessful candidate for president of the United States in 1872. When he died just a few weeks after his overwhelming defeat to Ulysses S. Grant that year, thousands thronged the streets of New York to mourn his passing.

But Greeley was above all a newspaperman, eloquent and influential in his editorials, meticulous as a reporter at large. Even as editor of the *Tribune*, he preferred to report important events himself rather than assign the task to a subordinate. So when the opportunity arose in the spring of 1859 for a journey across America to report on the mining boom in the West, he seized it at once. His dispatches to the East, promptly printed in the *Tribune*, were later gathered together to comprise a full account of the odyssey entitled *An Overland Journey*. Two of his reports from Colorado, dated June 9 and 21, are reprinted here, and describe the new-born city of Denver as well as life in the mountain mining camps.

THE KANSAS*
GOLD-DIGGINGS

In the Rocky Mountains,
Gregory's Diggings, June 9, 1859.

Wᴇ LEFT DENVER AT SIX
yesterday morning, in a wagon drawn by four mules, crossing immediately by a rope ferry the south fork of the Platte. This fork is a swift,
clear, cold stream, now several feet deep and some twenty rods wide,
but fordable except when snows are melting in the mountains. Many
gold-seekers' wagons were waiting to cross, and more were momently
arriving, so that the ferryman at least must be making his pile out of
the diggings. Henceforward, our way lay northwest for fifteen miles,
across a rolling and well-grassed prairie, on which one or two farms
had been commenced, while two or three persons have just established
"ranches"—that is, have built each his corral, in which cattle are herded
at night, while allowed to run at large on the prairie during the day:
$1.50 per month is the usual price per head for herding in this way,
and the cattle are said to do very well. The miners leave or send back
their cattle to herd on these prairies, while they prosecute their opera-
tions in the mountains where feed is generally scarce.

Reaching Clear Creek (properly Vasquer's Fork), a cold, swift, rocky-
bottomed stream, which emerges just above through a deep, narrow
canyon from the Rocky Mountains, we left our wagons, saddled the
mules and forded the creek (and it was all our mules could do to stem
its impetuous current), ascended a gentle, grassy slope to the foot of
the Rocky Mountains—which had for an hour seemed almost within

---

*So called because they lay in the central part of present Colorado, which was
Kansas Territory under the Kansas-Nebraska Act of 1854.

Fortune-seekers defying the elements to reach the Gregory Diggings during Colorado's Gold Rush.

a stone's throw on our left. Now they were to be faced directly, and the prospect was really serious. The hill on which we were to make our first essay in climbing, rose to a height of one thousand six hundred feet in a little more than a mile—the ascent for most of the distance being more than one foot in three. I never before saw teams forced up such a precipice; yet there were wagons with ten or twelve hundred weight of mining tools, bedding, provisions, etc., being dragged by four to eight yoke of oxen up that giddy precipice, with four or five men lifting at the wheels of each. The average time consumed in the ascent is some two hours. Our mules, unused to such work, were visibly appalled by it; at first they resisted every effort to force them up, even by zigzags. My companions all walked, but I was lame and had to ride, much to my mule's intense disgust. He was stubborn, but strong, and in time bore me safely to the summit.

New as this rugged road is—it was first traversed five weeks ago today—death had traveled it before me. A young man, shot dead while carelessly drawing a rifle from his wagon, lies buried by the roadside on this mountain. I have heard of so many accidents of this nature—not less than a dozen gold-seekers having been shot in this manner during the last two months—that I marvel at the carelessness with which firearms are everywhere handled on this side of the Missouri. Had no single emigrant across the Plains this season armed himself, the number of them alive at this moment would have been greater than it is.

We traveled some two miles along the crest of this mountain, then descended, by a pitch equally sharp with the ascent, but shorter, to a ravine, in which we rested our weary animals and dined. That dinner—of cold ham, bread and cheese—was one of the best relished of any I ever shared. Resaddling, we climbed another precipice a little less steep—and so up and down for ten miles, when we descended into the narrow valley of a little branch of Clear Creek, and thenceforward had ten miles of relatively smooth going, crossing from one valley to another over hills of moderate elevation and easy ascent.

A wilderness of mountains rose all around us, some higher, some lower, but generally very steep, with sharp, narrow ridges for their summits. Some of them are thinly grassed, between widely scattered trees up their sides and on their tops; but they are generally timbered, and mainly with yellow pine, some of it quite large, but more of it small and apparently young. High on the mountains, this pine is short and scraggy, while in the ravines it grows tall and shapely, but averages not more than a foot in diameter. Hurricanes have frequently swept these mountains, prostrating the pines by scores; fires have ravaged and decimated them; still, pines on the summits, pine on the hillsides, pines even in the ravines, are all but universal. The balsam fir grows sparingly in the ravines; hemlock, also, is reported, though I have not seen it: but the quaking asp or aspen—which seems but a more delicate species of cottonwood—is thick-set in the ravines, and sometimes appears on the more moderate acclivities, as do gooseberry bushes in the glens. Brooks of the purest water murmur and sing in every ravine; springs abound; the air is singularly pure and bracing; the elk, black-tailed deer and mountain sheep are plentiful, except where disturbed by the inrush of emigration; grouse are common and bold: the solitude was sylvan and perfect until a few weeks ago. All is now being rapidly changed, and not entirely for the better.

We had a smart shower, with thunder and lightning, during the afternoon, which compelled us to halt a few minutes. Another such this afternoon, indicates that it is a habit of the country. I am told, however, that though thunder is common, rain is generally withheld at this season, or confined to a mere sprinkle.

Night fell upon us, while yet six or seven miles from the diggings, and we camped in the edge of the pines, on the brow of a gentle acclivity, with a prospect of grass as well as water for our weary, hungry beasts down the slope south of us. Mine had fallen to her knees in the last watercourse we had passed, very nearly throwing me over her head; had she done it, I am sure I had not the strength left to rise and remount, and hardly to walk the remaining half mile. As it was, I had to be lifted tenderly from my saddle and laid on a blanket, with two more above me, where I lay while the fire was built, supper prepared, and a lodge of dry poles and green pine boughs hastily erected. I was too tired to eat, but the bright, leaping flame from the dry pines heaped on our fire gradually overcame the shivering, which was about the only sign of vitality I showed when first laid down, and I at length resumed the perpendicular by an effort, and took my place in our booth, where sleep but fitfully visited me during that bright, cool, short summer night. But this left me more time to rub my chafed and stiffened limbs, so that, when breakfast was called in the morning, I was ready, appetite included, and prepared to dispel the apprehensions of those who had predicted, on seeing me taken off my mule, that I must be left there for at least a day. By six o'clock, we were again in the saddle, and pushing on, over a stony but rather level tableland, which extended for two or three miles, thickly covered with young pines and aspens, to the next ravine, whence the road leads up a short, steep hill, then down a very long, equally steep one, to Ralston's Fork of Clear Creek—being as rapid and rock-bottomed as where we had crossed the main creek the day before thirty miles below, but with only one-third the volume of water, so that we forded it easily without a wet foot. A little runnel coming in from the west directly at the Ford, with its natural translucency changed to milky whiteness by the running of its waters through sluices in which the process of gold-washing was going forward, gave us assurance that we were in immediate proximity to the new but already famous workings called, after their discoverer, Gregory's Diggings.*

---

*Now known as Central City.

I shall not here speak of their pecuniary success or promise, though I have visited, during the day, a majority of those which have sluices already in operation, and received reports from my fellow visitors from nearly all the others. Having united with them in a statement—to be herewith forwarded—of what we saw and learned, I refer those who feel any interest in the matter to that statement. What I propose here to do is to give the reader some idea of the place and its general aspects.

The little brook which here joins Clear Creek from the west starts at the foot of mountains three or four miles distant, and runs in a usually narrow ravine between generally steep hills from five hundred to fifteen hundred feet high. Gregory's lead is very near its mouth; half a mile above seems the heart of the present mining region, though there are already sluices in operation at intervals for at least two miles up the runnel, and others are soon to be started at intervals above them. Three or four miles southwest from its mouth are Russell's Diggings, where coarse gold is procured, but I was unable to visit them. Prospecting is actively going forward in every direction, and vague reports of lucky hits or brilliant prospects are started on this side or on that, but I have not been able to verify them. It is no disparagement to the others to say that, though mining is carried on at various points within a radius of thirty miles from this spot, Gregory's Diggings are today the chief hope of gold-mining in the Rocky Mountains.

Six weeks ago, this ravine was a solitude, the favorite haunt of the elk, the deer, and other shy denizens of the profoundest wildernesses, seldom invaded by the footsteps of man. I believe this strip of country has long been debatable land between the Utes and the Arapahoes, which circumstances combined with its rarely accessible situation to secure its wild tenants against human intrusion and persecution. I hear that the Arapahoes say that a good "lodgepole trail"—that is, one which a pony may traverse with one end of the lodgepoles on his back, the other trailing behind him—exists from this point on to the open prairie where Clear Creek debouches from the mountains—a trail which doubtless winds along the steep sides of the ravines and avoids the rugged heights necessarily traversed by the miner's wagon road. Should these diggings justify their present promise, I doubt not a road will in time be made, reducing by one half—say five thousand feet—the present aggregate of ascent and descent between this and Denver. But an unworked wagon road must avoid the sides of these steep-banked ravines, running square up the faces and along the crests of the mountains, so that this spot is destined to remain barely accessible for at least another year.

This narrow valley is densely wooded, mainly with the inevitable yellow pine, which, sheltered from the fierce winds which sweep the mountaintops, here grows to a height of sixty or eighty feet, though usually but a foot to eighteen inches in diameter. Of these pines, log cabins are constructed with extreme facility, and probably one hundred are now being built, while three or four hundred more are in immediate contemplation. They are covered with the green boughs of the pines, then with earth, and bid fair to be commodious and comfortable. As yet, the entire population of the valley—which cannot number less than four thousand, including five white women and seven squaws living with white men—sleep in tents, or under booths of pine boughs, cooking and eating in the open air. I doubt that there is as yet a table or chair in these diggings, eating being done around a cloth spread on the ground, while each one sits or reclines on mother earth. The food, like that of the Plains, is restricted to a few staples—pork, hot bread, beans and coffee forming the almost exclusive diet of the mountains; but a meatshop has just been established, on whose altar are offered up the ill-fed and well-whipped oxen who are just in from a fifty days' journey across the plains, and one or two cows have been driven in, as more would be if they could here been subsisted. But these mountains are mainly wooded, while the open hillsides are so dry during summer that their grass is very scanty. It is melancholy to see so many over-worked and half-starved cattle as one meets or passes in this ravine and on the way hither. Corn is four dollars per bushel in Denver, and scarce at that; oats are not to be had; there is not a ton of hay within two hundred miles, and none can ever be brought hither over the present road at a cost below forty dollars per ton. The present shift of humane owners is to herd their oxen or mules on the rich grass of the nearest prairies for a week or so, then bring them in here and keep them at work for a week or more, letting them subsist on browse and a very little grass, and then send them down the mountain again. This, bad as it is, seems the best that can be done. Living of all kinds will always be dear at these mines, where American flour is now selling at the rate of forty-four dollars per barrel, and bacon is worth fifty cents per pound; sugar ditto.

I presume less than half the four or five thousand people now in this ravine have been here a week; he who has been here three weeks is regarded as quite an old settler. The influx cannot fall short of five hundred per day, balanced by an efflux of about one hundred. Many of the latter go away convinced that Rocky Mountain gold-mining is one grand humbug. Some of them have prospected two or three weeks, eating up their provisions, wearing out their boots—and finding nothing. Others have worked for the more fortunate for one dollar per day and their board and lodging—certainly not high wages when the quality of the living is considered. And I feel certain that, while some—perhaps many—will realize their dreams of wealth here, a far greater number will expend their scanty means, tax their powers of endurance, and then leave, soured, heartsick, spirit-broken. Twenty thousand people will have rushed into this ravine before the 1st of September, while I do not see how half of them are to find profitable employment here. Unless, therefore, the area of the diggings shall meantime be greatly enlarged—of which there is no assurance—I cannot imagine how half the number are to subsist here, even up to that early setting in of winter which must cause a general paralysis of mining, and consequently of all other Rocky Mountain industry. With the gold just wrested from the earth still glittering in my eyes—and one company has taken out today, at a cost of not more than twenty-five dollars, a lump (condensed by the use of quicksilver) which looks like a steelyard poise and is estimated as worth five hundred and ten dollars—I adhere to my long-settled conviction that, next to outright and indisputable gambling, the hardest (though sometimes the quickest) way to obtain gold is to mine for it; that a good farmer or mechanic will usually make money faster, and of course immeasurably easier, by sticking to his own business than by deserting it for gold-digging; and that the man who, having failed in some other pursuit, calculates on retrieving his fortunes by gold-mining, makes a mistake which he will be likely to rue to the end of his days.

We had a famous gathering a few rods from this tent this evening. The estimate of safe men puts the number present at fifteen hundred to two thousand. Though my name was made the excuse for it, brief and forcible addresses were made by several others, wherein mining, postal, and express facilities, the Pacific railroad, the proposed new Rocky Mountain State, temperance, gambling, etc., etc., were discussed with force and freedom. Such a gathering of men suddenly drawn hither from every section, and nearly every state, in a glen where the first axe was raised, the first tent pitched by white men, less than six weeks ago, should have inspired the dullest speaker with earnestness, if not with eloquence.

Mining quickens almost every department of useful industry. Two coal pits are burning close at hand. A blacksmith has set up his forge here, and is making a good thing of sharpening picks at fifty cents each. A volunteer post office is just established, to which an express office will soon attach itself. A provision store will soon follow, then groceries, then dry goods, then a hotel, etc., until within ten years the tourist of the continent will be whirled up to these diggings over a longer but far easier road winding around the mountaintops rather than passing over them, and will sip his chocolate and read his New York paper— not yet five days old—at the Gregory House, in utter unconsciousness that this region was wrested from the elk and the mountain sheep so recently as 1859.

The vigilant prospector.

Denver, June 10, 1859.

We left the diggings yesterday morning, and came down to the foot
of the mountains, in spite of a drizzling rain from noon to three or
four o'clock, which at one time threatened a heavy shower. We made
a poor shelter of a buffalo skin and a rubber blanket, stretched across
a fallen tree, and there waited half an hour; but, finding the rain neither
stopped nor grew violent, we saddled up and came on. Two accidents,
which might have proved serious, happened to members of our party —
the first to Mr. Villard, of Cincinnati, who, riding at some distance
from all others, was thrown by his mule's saddle slipping forward and
turning under him, so that he fell heavily on his left arm, which was
badly bruised, and thence was dragged a rod with his heel fast in the
stirrup. His mule then stopped; but when I rode up behind him, I dared
not approach him lest I should start her, and waited a moment for the
friend who, having heard his call for help, was coming up in front. Mr.
V. was released without further injury, but his arm is temporarily useless. The other casualty happened to Mr. Kershaw, of New York, who,
riding to my assistance at Clear Creek crossing at nightfall, was thrown
by his mule's starting at the rush of a savage dog, and considerably
injured, though he is nearly well today. It would have been to me a
source of lasting sorrow had his fall resulted in more serious damage.

When we reached Clear Creek on our way up three mornings since,
though the current rushing from the mountains looked somewhat formidable, I charged it like a Zouave, and was greeted with three ringing
shouts from the assembled Pike's Peakers, as I came up, gay and dripping, on the north shore. But now, though the water was but a few
inches higher, the starch was so completely taken out of me by those
three days' rough experience in the mountains, that I had neither strength
nor heart for the passage. I felt that the least stumble of my mule over
the round, slippery stones that fill the channel would fling me, and that
I was unable to stand a moment in that rushing torrent. So, driving
in my mule after the rest of the party, and seeing her reach the south
bank safely, though with great difficulty—breaking a girth and spilling
saddle, blanket, etc., into the water—I betook myself to a spot, half
a mile upstream, where the creek is split by islets into three channels,
and where a rude footbridge of logs affords a dry-shod passage. Here
I was met by my friend with his mule, and in a few minutes rode to
our wagon, beside which we found supper in an emigrant tent and lodging in several, at four o'clock this morning harnessed up and drove into

Denver—just three whole men out of a party of six, and all as weary and care-worn as need be, but all heartily gratified with our experience of three days in the Rocky Mountains.

WESTERN CHARACTERS

Denver, June 21, 1859.

I know it is not quite correct to speak of this region as "Western," seeing that it is in fact the center of North America and very close to its backbone. Still, as the terms "Eastern" and "Western" are conventional and relative—Castine being "Western" to a Bluenose, and Carson Valley "Eastern" to a Californian—I take the responsibility of grouping certain characters I have noted on the Plains and in or about the mountains as "Western," begging that most respectable region which lies east of the buffalo range—also that portion which lies west of the Colorado—to excuse the liberty.

The first circumstance that strikes a stranger traversing this wild country is the vagrant instincts and habits of the great majority of its denizens—perhaps I should say, of the American people generally, as exhibited here. Among any ten whom you successively meet, there will be natives of New England, New York, Pennsylvania, Virginia or Georgia, Ohio or Indiana, Kentucky or Missouri, France, Germany, and perhaps Ireland. But, worse than this; you cannot enter a circle of a dozen persons of whom at least three will not have spent some years in California, two or three have made claims and built cabins in Kansas or Nebraska, and at least one spent a year or so in Texas. Boston, New York, Philadelphia, New Orleans, St. Louis, Cincinnati, have all contributed their quota toward peopling the new gold region. The next man you meet driving an ox team, and white as a miller with dust, is probably an ex-banker or doctor, a broken merchant or manufacturer from the old states, who has scraped together the candle ends charitably or contemptuously allowed him by his creditors on settlement, and risked them on a last desperate cast of the dice by coming hither. Ex-editors, ex-printers, ex-clerks, ex-steamboat men, are here in abundance—all on the keen hunt for the gold which only a few will secure. One of the stations at which we slept on our way up—a rough tent with a cheering hope (since blasted) of a log house in the near future—was kept by an ex-lawyer of Cincinnati and his wife, an ex-actress from our New York Bowery—she being cook. Omnibus drivers from Broadway repeatedly handled the ribbons; ex-border ruffians from civilized Kansas—some of them of unblessed memory—were encountered on our way, at intervals none too long. All these, blended with veteran mountain men, Indians of all grades from the tamest to the wildest, half-breeds, French trappers and *voyageurs* (who have generally two or three Indian wives apiece), and an occasional Negro, compose a medley such as hardly another region can parallel. Honolulu, or some other port of the South Sea Islands, could probably match it most nearly.

The old mountaineers form a caste by themselves, and they prize the distinction. Some of them are Frenchmen, or Franco-Americans, who have been trapping or trading in and around these mountains for a quarter of a century, have wives and children here, and here expect to live and die. Some of these have accumulated property and cash to the value of two hundred thousand dollars, which amount will not easily be reduced, as they are frugal in everything (liquor sometimes excepted), spend but a pittance on the clothing of their families, trust little, keep small stocks of goods, and sell at large profits. Others came years ago from the states, some of them on account each of a "difficulty" wherein they severally killed or savagely maimed their respective antagonists under circumstances on which the law refuses to look leniently; whence their pilgrimage to and prolonged sojourn here, despite enticing placards offering five hundred dollars or perhaps one thousand dollars for their safe return to the places that knew them once, but shall know them no more. This class is not numerous, but is more influential than it should be in giving tone to the society of which its members form a part. Prone to deep drinking, soured in temper, always armed, bristling at a word, ready with the rifle, revolver or bowie knife, they give law and set fashions which, in a country where the regular administration of justice is yet a matter of prophecy, it seems difficult to overrule or disregard. I apprehend that there have been, during my two weeks' sojourn, more brawls, more fights, more pistol shots with criminal intent in this log city of one hundred and fifty dwellings, not three-fourths completed nor two-thirds inhabited, nor one-third fit to be, than in any community of no greater numbers on earth. This will be changed in time—I trust within a year, for the empty houses are steadily find- ing tenants from the two streams of emigration rolling in daily up the Platte on the one hand, down Cherry Creek on the other, including some scores of women and children, who generally stop here, as all of them should; for life in the mountains is yet horribly rough. Public religious worship, a regular mail and other civilizing influences, are being established; there is a gleam of hope that the Arapahoes—who have made the last two or three nights indescribably hideous by their infernal war whoops, songs and dances—will at last clear out on the foray against the Utes they have so long threatened, diminishing largely the aggregate of drunkenness and riot, and justifying expectations of comparative peace. So let me close up my jottings from this point—which circumstances beyond my control have rendered so voluminous—with a rough ambrotype of

LIFE IN DENVER

The rival cities of Denver and Auraria front on each other from either bank of Cherry Creek, just before it is lost in the South Platte. The Platte has its sources in and around the South Park of the Rocky Mountains, a hundred miles southwest of this point; but Cherry Creek is headed off from them by that river, and, winding its northward course of forty or fifty miles over the Plains, with its sources barely touching the mountains, is a capricious stream, running quite smartly when we came here, but whose broad and thirsty sands have since drank it all up at this point, leaving the log footbridges which connect the two cities as useless as an icehouse in November. The Platte, aided by the melting of the snows on the higher mountains, runs nearly full-banked, though the constant succession of hot suns and dry winds begins to tell upon it; while Clear Creek (properly Vasquez's Fork), which issues directly from the mountains just above its crossing on the way to the Gregory diggings, is nearly at its highest, and will so remain till the inner mountains are mainly denuded of their snowy mantles. But, within a few days, a footbridge has been completed over the Platte, virtually abolishing the ferry and saving considerable time and money to gold-seekers and travelers; while another over Clear Creek precludes not only delay but danger—several wagons having been wrecked and two or three men all but drowned in attempts to ford its rapid, rocky current. Thus the ways of the adventurous grow daily smoother; and they who visit this region ten years hence will regard as idle tales the stories of privation, impediment, and "hairbreadth'scapes" which are told, or might be, by the gold-seekers of 1859.

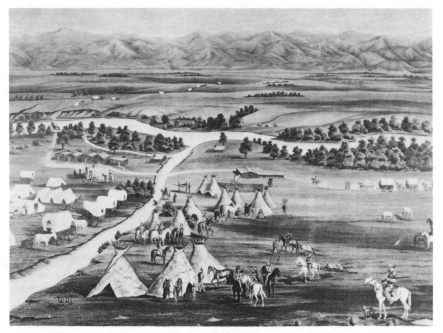

The confluence of Cherry Creek and the South Platte River—Denver, 1859.

Of these rival cities, Auraria is by far the more venerable—some of its structures being, I think, fully a year old, if not more. Denver, on the other hand, can boast of no antiquity beyond September or October last. In the architecture of the two cities there is, notwithstanding, a striking similarlity—cottonwood logs, cut from the adjacent bottom of the Platte, roughly hewed on the upper and under sides, and chinked with billets of split cottonwood on the inner, and with mud on the outer side, forming the walls of nearly or quite every edifice which adorns either city. Across the center of the interior, from shorter wall to wall, stretches a sturdy ridgepole, usually in a state of nature, from which "shooks," or split saplings of cottonwood, their split sides down, incline gently to the transverse or longer sides; on these (in the more finished structures) a coating of earth is laid; and, with a chimney of mud-daubed sticks in one corner, a door nearly opposite, and a hole beside it representing or prefiguring a window, the edifice is complete. Of course, many have no earth on their covering of shooks, and so are liable to gentle inundation in the rainy season; but, though we have had thunder and lightning almost daily, with a brisk gale in most instances, there has been no rain worth naming such here for weeks, and the unchinked, barely shook-covered houses, through whose sides and roofs you may see the stars as you lie awake nights, are decidedly the cooler and airier. There is a new hotel nearly finished in Auraria, which has a second-story (but no first-story) floor; beside this, mine eyes have never yet been blessed with the sight of any floor whatever in either Denver or Auraria. The last time I slept or ate with a floor under me (our wagon box and mother earth excepted) was at Junction City, nearly four weeks ago. The Denver House, which is the Astor House of the gold region, has walls of logs, a floor of earth, with windows and roof of rather flimsy cotton sheeting; while every guest is allowed as good a bed as his blankets will make. The charges are no higher than at the Astor and other first-class hotels, except for liquor— twenty-five cents a drink for dubious whisky, colored and nicknamed to suit the taste of customers, being the regular rate throughout this region. I had the honor to be shaved there by a nephew (so he assured me) of Murat, Bonaparte's king of Naples—the honor and the shave together costing but a paltry dollar. Still, a few days of such luxury surfeited me, mainly because the main or drinking room was also occupied by several blacklegs as a gambling hall, and their incessant clamor of "Who'll go me twenty? The ace of hearts is the winning card. Whoever turns the ace of hearts wins the twenty dollars," etc., etc., persisted in at all hours up to midnight, became at length a nuisance, from which I craved deliverance at any price. Then the visitors of that drinking and gambling room had a careless way, when drunk, of firing revolvers, sometimes at each other, at other times quite miscellaneously, which struck me as inconvenient for a quiet guest with only a leg and a half, hence in poor condition for dodging bullets. So I left.

"How do you live in Denver?" I inquired of a New York friend some weeks domiciled here, in whose company I visited the mines. "O, I've jumped a cabin," was his cool, matter-of-course reply. As jumping a cabin was rather beyond my experience, I inquired further, and learned that, finding an uninhabited cabin that suited him, he had quietly entered and spread his blankets, eating at home or abroad as opportunity might suggest. I found, on further inquiry, that at least one-third of the inhabitations in Denver and Auraria were desolate when we came here (they have been gradually filling up since), some of the owners having gone into the mountains, digging or prospecting, and taken their limited supply of household goods along with them; while others, discouraged by the poor show of mining six weeks ago, when even the nearer mountains were still covered with snow and ice, rushed pell-mell down the Platte with the wild reflux of the spring emigration, abandoning all but what they could carry away. It is said that lots and cabins together sold for twenty-five dollars—so long as there were purchasers; but these soon failing, they were left behind like campfires in the morning, and have since been at the service of all comers.

So, in company with a journalizing friend, I, too, have "jumped a cabin," and have kept to it quite closely, under a doctor's care, for the last week or ten days. It is about ten feet square, and eight feet high, rather too well chinked for summer, considering that it lacks a window, but must be a capital house for this country in winter. I board with the nearest neighbor; and it is not my landlady's fault that the edible resources of Denver are decidedly limited. But even these are improving. To the bread, bacon, and beans, which formed the staple of every meal a short time ago, there have been several recent additions; milk, which was last week twenty-five cents per quart, is now down to ten, and I hear a rumor that eggs, owing to a recent increase in the number of hens, within five hundred miles, from four or five to twelve or fifteen, are about to fall from a dollar a dozen to fifty cents per dozen. On every side, I note signs of progress—improvement—manifest destiny: there was a man about the city yesterday with lettuce to sell, and I am credibly assured that there will be green peas next month—actually peas!—provided it should rain soakingly meantime—whereof a hazy, lowering sky would seem just now to afford some hope. (P. S. The hope has vanished.) But I—already sadly behind, and nearly able to travel again—must turn my back on this promise of luxuries, and take the road to Laramie today, or at furthest tomorrow.

MARK TWAIN.

1861

Throughout his long life, Mark Twain had only two known encounters with the people of Colorado. The first occurred in 1861, when the young humorist was, like his predecessor Francis Parkman, undertaking a journey across the West that would later be chronicled in a popular book. But *Roughing It,* Twain's lively account of a stagecoach trip from St. Joseph, Missouri to San Francisco, departed significantly from the sober narrative of *The Oregon Trail.* For Twain was not so much awed by the geography of the West as he was amused by the behavior of its inhabitants; throughout what must have been an arduous journey across a great deal of hostile territory, Twain kept his eyes peeled for the peculiarities of western characters—particularly those of questionable moral integrity.

Such was Twain's fancy when his party bisected the extreme northeastern section of Colorado just five days out of St. Joseph. Their "mudwagon" having broken down some eighty miles west of Julesburg, Twain and his fellow passengers resorted to buffalo hunting to bide the time until the coach was repaired. In the pages that follow, Twain recounts the sad tale of a passenger named Bemis, who returned to the encampment horseless and weary from the chase, and whose alibi Twain found highly improbable, but somehow typical of human nature.

Twain's second brush with Coloradans occurred forty-one years later, when the aging writer learned that the Denver Public Library had just removed *Huckleberry Finn* from its shelves at the request of some clergymen who found the book offensive. Sensing an opportunity to inspire some classic invective, *The Denver Post* wired Twain and asked for his reaction to the banning. His response, printed against his will in the *Post,* follows the selection from *Roughing It.*

ROUGHING IT
IN COLORADO

At NOON ON THE FIFTH day out, we arrived at the "Crossing of the South Platte," *alias* "Julesburg," *alias* "Overland City," four hundred and seventy miles from St. Joseph— the strangest, quaintest, funniest frontier town that our untraveled eyes had ever stared at and been astonished with.

It did seem strange enough to see a town again after what appeared to us such a long acquaintance with deep, still, almost lifeless and house- less solitude! We tumbled out into the busy street feeling like meteoric people crumbled off the corner of some other world, and wakened up suddenly in this. For an hour we took as much interest in Overland City as if we had never seen a town before. The reason we had an hour to spare was because we had to change our stage (for a less sumptuous affair, called a "mud-wagon") and transfer our freight of mails.

Presently we got under way again. We came to the shallow, yellow, muddy South Platte, with its low banks and its scattering flat sand-bars and pygmy islands—a melancholy stream straggling through the center of the enormous flat plain, and only saved from being impossible to find with the naked eye by its sentinel rank of scattering trees standing on either bank. The Platte was "up," they said—which made me wish I could see it when it was down, if it could look any sicker and sorrier. They said it was a dangerous stream to cross, now, because its quick- sands were liable to swallow up horses, coach, and passengers if an attempt was made to ford it. But the mails had to go, and we made the attempt. Once or twice in midstream the wheels sunk into the yielding sands so threateningly that we half believed we had dreaded and avoided the sea all our lives to be shipwrecked in a "mud-wagon" in the middle of a desert at last. But we dragged through and sped away toward the setting sun.

Next morning just before dawn, when about five hundred and fifty miles from St. Joseph, our mud-wagon broke down. We were to be delayed five or six hours, and therefore we took horses, by invitation, and joined a party who were just starting on a buffalo-hunt. It was noble sport galloping over the plain in the dewy freshness of the morning, but our part of the hunt ended in disaster and disgrace, for a wounded buffalo bull chased the passenger Bemis nearly two miles, and then he forsook his horse and took to a lone tree. He was very sullen about the matter for some twenty-four hours, but at last he began to soften little by little, and finally he said:

"Well, it was not funny, and there was no sense in those gawks making themselves so facetious over it. I tell you I was angry in earnest for a while. I should have shot that long gangly lubber they called Hank, if I could have done it without crippling six or seven other people— but of course I couldn't, the old 'Allen' 's so confounded comprehensive. I wish those loafers had been up in the tree; they wouldn't have wanted to laugh so. If I had had a horse worth a cent—but no, the minute he saw that buffalo bull wheel on him and give a bellow, he raised straight up in the air and stood on his heels. The saddle began to slip, and I took him round the neck and laid close to him, and began to pray. Then he came down and stood up on the other end awhile, and the bull actually stopped pawing sand and bellowing to contemplate the inhuman spectacle. Then the bull made a pass at him and uttered a bellow that sounded perfectly frightful, it was so close to me, and that seemed to literally prostrate my horse's reason, and make a raving distracted maniac of him, and I wish I may die if he didn't stand on his head for a quarter of a minute and shed tears. He was absolutely out of his mind—he was, as sure as truth itself, and he really didn't know what he was doing. Then the bull came charging at us, and my horse dropped down on all fours and took a fresh start—and then for the next ten minutes he would actually throw one handspring after another so fast that the bull began to get unsettled, too, and didn't know where to start in—and so he stood there sneezing, and shoveling dust over his back, and bellowing every now and then, and thinking he had got a fifteen-hundred-dollar circus horse for breakfast, certain. Well, I was first out on his neck—the horse's, not the bull's—and then underneath, and next on his rump, and sometimes head up, and sometimes heels— but I tell you it seemed solemn and awful to be ripping and tearing and carrying on so in the presence of death, as you might say. Pretty soon the bull made a snatch for us and brought away some of my horse's tail (I suppose, but do not know, being pretty busy at the time), but *something* made him hungry for solitude and suggested to him to get up and hunt for it. And then you ought to have seen that spider-legged old skeleton go! and you ought to have seen the bull cut out after him, too—head down, tongue out, tail up, bellowing like everything, and actually mowing down the weeds, and tearing up the earth, and boosting up the sand like a whirlwind! By George, it was a hot race! I and the saddle were back on the rump, and I had the bridle in my teeth and holding on to the pommel with both hands. First we left the dogs behind; then we passed a jackass-rabbit; then we overtook a coyote, and were gaining on an antelope when the rotten girths let go and threw me about thirty yards off to the left, and as the saddle went down over the horse's rump he gave it a lift with his heels that sent it more than four hundred yards up in the air, I wish I may die in a minute if he didn't. I fell at the foot of the only solitary tree there was in nine counties adjacent (as any creature could see with the naked eye), and the next second I had hold of the bark with four sets of nails and my teeth, and the next second after that I was astraddle of the main limb and blaspheming my luck in a way that made my breath smell of brimstone. I *had* the bull, now, if he did not think of *one* thing. But that one thing I dreaded. I dreaded it very seriously. There was a possibility that the bull might not think of it, but there were greater changes that he would. I made up my mind what I would do in case he did. It was a little over forty feet to the ground from where I sat. I cautiously unwound the lariat from the pommel of my saddle—"

"Your *saddle?* Did you take your saddle up in the tree with you?"

"Take it up in the tree with me? Why, how you talk! Of course I didn't. No man could do that. It *fell* in the tree when it came down."

"Oh—exactly."

"Certainly. I unwound the lariat, and fastened one end of it to the limb. It was the very best green rawhide, and capable of sustaining tons. I made a slip-noose in the other end, and then hung it down to see the length. It reached down twenty-two feet—half-way to the ground. I then loaded every barrel of the Allen with a double charge. I felt satisfied. I said to myself, if he never thinks of that one thing that I dread, all right—but if he does, all right anyhow—I am fixed for him. But don't you know that the very thing a man dreads is the thing that always happens? Indeed it is so. I watched the bull, now, with anxiety—anxiety

which no one can conceive of who has not been in such a situation
and felt that at any moment death might come. Presently a thought
came into the bull's eye. I knew it! said I—if my nerve fails now, I am
lost. Sure enough, it was just as I had dreaded, he started in to climb
the tree—"

"What, the bull?"

"Of course—who else?"

"But a bull can't climb a tree."

"He can't, can't he? Since you know so much about it, did you ever
see a bull try?"

"No! I never dreamt of such a thing."

"Well, then, what is the use of your talking that way, then? Because
you never saw a thing done, is that any reason why it can't be done?"

"Well, all right—go on. What did you do?"

"The bull started up, and got along well for about ten feet, then
slipped and slid back. I breathed easier. He tried it again—got up a little
higher—slipped again. But he came at it once more, and this time he
was careful. He got gradually higher and higher, and my spirits went
down more and more. Up he came—an inch at a time—with his eyes
hot, and his tongue hanging out. Higher and higher—hitched his foot

over the stump of a limb, and looked up, as much as to say, 'You are my meat, friend.' Up again—higher and higher, and getting more excited the closer he got. He was within ten feet of me! I took a long breath— and then said I, 'It is now or never.' I had the coil of the lariat all ready; I paid it out slowly, till it hung right over his head; all of a sudden I let go of the slack and the slip-noose fell fairly round his neck! Quicker than lightning I out with the Allen and let him have it in the face. It was an awful roar, and must have scared the bull out of his senses. When the smoke cleared away, there he was, dangling in the air, twenty foot from the ground, and going out of one convulsion into another faster than you could count! I didn't stop to count, anyhow—I shinned down the tree and shot for home."

"Bemis, is all that true, just as you have stated it?"

"I wish I may rot in my tracks and die the death of a dog if it isn't."

"Well, we can't refuse to believe it, and we don't. But if there were some proofs—"

"Proofs! Did I bring back my lariat?"

"No."

"Did I bring back my horse?"

"No."

"Did you ever see the bull again?"

"No."

"Well, then, what more do you want? I never saw anybody as particular as you are about a little thing like that."

I made up my mind that if this man was not a liar he only missed it by the skin of his teeth. This episode reminds me of an incident of my brief sojourn in Siam, years afterward. The European citizens of a town in the neighborhood of Bangkok had a prodigy among them by the name of Eckert, an Englishman—a person famous for the number, ingenuity, and imposing magnitude of his lies. They were always repeating his most celebrated falsehoods, and always trying to "draw him out" before strangers; but they seldom succeeded. Twice he was invited to the house where I was visiting, but nothing could seduce him into a specimen lie. One day a planter named Bascom, an influential man, and a proud and sometimes irascible one, invited me to ride over with him and call on Eckert. As we jogged along, said he:

"Now, do you know where the fault lies? It lies in putting Eckert on his guard. The minute the boys go to pumping at Eckert he knows perfectly well what they are after, and of course he shuts up his shell.

Anybody might know he would. But when we get there, we must play him finer than that. Let him shape the conversation to suit himself— let him drop it or change it whenever he wants to. Let him see that nobody is trying to draw him out. Just let him have his own way. He will soon forget himself and begin to grind out lies like a mill. Don't get impatient—just keep quiet, and let me play him. I will make him lie. It does seem to me that the boys must be blind to overlook such an obvious and simple trick as that."

Eckert received us heartily—a pleasant-spoken, gentle-mannered creature. We sat in the veranda an hour, sipping English ale, and talking about the king, and the sacred white elephant, the Sleeping Idol, and all manner of things; and I noticed that my comrade never led the conversation himself or shaped it, but simply followed Eckert's lead, and betrayed no solicitude and no anxiety about anything. The effect was shortly perceptible. Eckert began to grow communicative; he grew more and more talkative and sociable. Another hour passed in the same way, and then all of a sudden Eckert said:

"Oh, by the way! I came near forgetting. I have got a thing here to astonish you. Such a thing as neither you nor any other man ever heard of—I've got a cat that will eat cocoanut! Common green cocoanut—and not only eat the meat, but drink the milk. It is so—I'll swear to it."

A quick glance from Bascom—a glance that I understood—then:

"Why, bless my soul, I never heard of such a thing. Man, it is impossible."

"I knew you would say it. I'll fetch the cat."

He went in the house. Bascom said:

"There—what did I tell you? Now, that is the way to handle Eckert. You see, I have petted him along patiently, and put his suspicions to sleep. I am glad we came. You tell the boys about it when you go back. Cat eat a cocoanut—oh, my! Now, that is just his way, exactly—he will tell the absurdest lie, and trust to luck to get out of it again. Cat eat a cocoanut—the innocent fool!"

Eckert approached with his cat, sure enough.

Bascom smiled. Said he:

"I'll hold the cat—you bring a cocoanut."

Eckert split one open, and chopped up some pieces. Bascom smuggled a wink to me, and proffered a slice of the fruit to puss. She snatched it, swallowed it ravenously, and asked for more!

We rode our two miles in silence, and wide apart. At least I was silent, though Bascom cuffed his horse and cursed him a good deal, notwithstanding the horse was behaving well enough. When I branched off homeward, Bascom said:

"Keep the horse till morning. And—you need not speak of this ————— foolishness to the boys."

From The Denver Post, *August 14, 1902.*

MARK TWAIN SCORES.

Some Individuals Who Don't Like "Huckleberry Finn."

The Denver Post, on hearing that "Huckleberry Finn" had been thrown out of the Denver public library, wired to Mark Twain for an opinion on the subject. The Post received the letter herewith printed but it must add that the efforts of certain individuals to have the book discarded have failed and "Huckleberry Finn" will again adorn the shelves of the Denver public library as soon as the appropriation will permit its purchase. Mark Twain's letter is as follows:

MARK TWAIN'S LETTER.

Your telegram reached me (per post) from "York Village" (which is a short brickbat throw from my house) yesterday afternoon when it was 30 hours old. And yet, in my experience, that was not only abnormally quick work for a telegraph company to do, but abnormally intelligent work for that kind of mummy to be whirling off out of its alleged mind.

Twenty-four hours earlier the Country club had notified me that a stranger in Portsmouth (a half-hour from here) wished me to come to the club at 7.30 p.m., and call him up and talk upon a matter of business. I said: "Let him take the trolley and come over, if his business is worth the time and fare to him." It was doubtless yourself—and not in Portsmouth, but in Denver. I was not thinking much about business at the time, for the reason that a consultation of physicians was appointed for that hour (7.30) at my house to consider if means might be devised to save my wife's life. At the present writing—Thursday afternoon—it is believed that she will recover.

When the watch was relieved an hour ago and I left the sick chamber to take my respite I began to frame answers to your dispatch, but it was only to entertain myself, for I am aware that I am not privileged to speak freely in this matter, funny as the occasion is and dearly as I should like to laugh at it; and when I can't speak freely I don't speak at all.

You see, there are two or three pointers:

First—Huck Finn was turned out of a New England library 17 years ago—ostensibly on account of its morals; really to curry favor with a parsonage. There has been no other instance until now.

Second—A few months ago I published an article which threw mud at that pinch-beck hero, Funston,* and his extraordinary morals.

Third—Huck's morals have stood the strain in Denver and in every English, German and French speaking community in the world—save one—for seventeen years until now.

Fourth—The strain breaks the connection now.

Fifth—In Denver alone.

Sixth—Funston commands there.

Seventh—And he has dependants and influence.

When one puts these things together the cat that is in the meal is disclosed—and quite unmistakably.

Said cat consists of a few persons who wish to curry favor with Funston, and whom God has not dealt kindly with in the matter of wisdom.

Everybody in Denver knows this, even the dead people in the cemeteries. It may be that Funston has wit enough to know that these good idiots are adding another howling absurdity to his funny history; it may be that God has charitably spared him that degree of penetration, slight as it is; in any case he is—as usual—a proper object of comparison, and the bowels of my sympathy are moved toward him.

There's nobody for me to attack in this matter even with soft and gentle ridicule—and I shouldn't ever think of using a grown-up weapon in this kind of a nursery. Above all, I couldn't venture to attack the

---

*The reference is to General Frederick Funston, whom Twain satirized in an essay entitled "In Defense of Funston." Funston was largely responsible for an American imperial adventure in the Philippines in 1901.

clergymen whom you mention for I have their habits and live in the same glass house which they are occupying. I am always reading immoral books on the sly and then selfishly to prevent other people from having the same wicked good time.

No, if Satan's morals and Funston's are preferable to Huck's, let Huck's take a back seat; they can stand any ordinary competition, but not a combination like that. And I'm going to defend them anyway.

Sincerely yours,

S. L. Clemens.

York Harbor, Aug. 14, 1902.

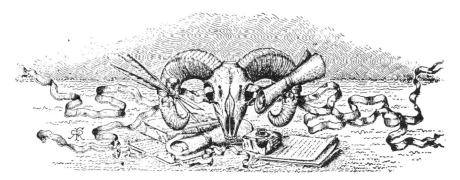

SAMUEL BOWLES.

Schuyler Colfax

Wm. Bross   *Saml Bowles*

1868

Colorado's potential for a healthy tourist industry was not overlooked even in the territorial period, when the primary attraction was the area's great mineral wealth. One of the most influential books of the time that described Colorado's possibilities as a resort suggested by its title, *The Switzerland of America,* a comparison to the geographic wonders of Europe.

The author of *The Switzerland of America* was Samuel Bowles, whose eminence as editor of the influential abolitionist newspaper Springfield (Mass.) *Republican* made him one of the leaders of American public opinion for nearly two decades. In fact, such was his stature in the years following the Civil War that his travelling companions for his Colorado adventures were none other than the vice-president of the United States and the lieutenant-governor of Illinois. Their guide for the trip over Berthoud Pass and into Middle Park was one of the territory's most prominent "boosters"—*Rocky Mountain News* founder William Byers.

In the following selection from *The Switzerland of America* it is apparent that Bowles showed foresight, if not prophecy, in identifying certain parts of the future state "where I would advise all pleasure travellers to Colorado to come." For from the top of Berthoud Pass (where this chronicle begins) Bowles lauds none other than the future site of one of Denver's mountain parks, the Winter Park ski area. In order to show that Bowles's visit to Colorado was not all merriment, however, a brief account of an "Indian scare" that occurred later in the trip follows the Middle Park chapter.

THE
MIDDLE PARK
AND AN
INDIAN SCARE

Hot Springs, Middle Park, August, 1868.

AFTER THREE OR FOUR
hours' hard riding, from the upper Clear Creek, we suddenly came out
of the trees into an open space of hardy green, bordered by snow, a
gap or sag in the mountains,—and behold we are at the top of Berthoud
Pass. The waters of the Atlantic and Pacific start from our very feet;
the winds from the two oceans suck through here into each other's
embrace; above us the mountain peaks go up sharp with snow and rock,
and shut in our view; but below and beyond through wide and thick
forests lies Middle Park, a varied picture of plain and hill, with snowy
peaks beyond and around. To this point, at least, I would advise all
pleasure travelers to Colorado to come; it is a feasible excursion for
any one who can sit in the saddle; it can be easily made with return
in a day from Empire, Georgetown or even Idaho; and it offers as much
of varied and sublime beauty in mountain scenery, as any so comparatively easy a trip yet within our experience possibly can.

But to follow us down into the Park is another and tougher affair;
the Colorado ladies do it occasionally, but it needs real strength and
endurance and an unfaltering enthusiasm. The descent is sharp and
rocky, and thick with timber, and worse, wet and miry. Bayard Taylor,
who came over in June, found the path heavy with snow, and impassable
to any but heroic travelers; now the snows are gone, and it is dryer

than at any other season, but it is a rough and hard descent, almost perpendicular in steepness at times, and full of treacherous holes of water and mire. But we all got through without disaster, and found relief about two o'clock in an open, grassy meadow, with a trout brook on its border. The order to camp was grateful; animals were turned loose, and we lolled in the sunshine, made and drank coffee, and ate our lunch of bread and butter, ham and canned peaches.

But we were not in the Park yet, and after an hour's rest, we remounted and moved on,—on, on, the road seemed interminable, through thick woods, over frequent morass and occasional mountain stream; deceptive in glimpse of park that was not the Park; all, save our irrepressible mountain leaders, weary with the long, rough ride, and eager for the end. It was near dark, after traveling from twenty to twenty-five miles in all, when we stopped for the night, in the woods, just without the open section of the Park. A bit of meadow with tall grass was at hand for the animals, and, relieved of saddles and packs, away they went, without let or hindrance, to enjoy it. The only precaution taken is to leave the lariat, a rope of twenty to thirty feet long, dragging at their necks, by which to catch them the more easily in the morning. Only a portion of the herd are thus provided, however. They rarely stray away far from camp; and if they should, these people make little of an hour or two's hunt to find them, which they are quite sure of doing wherever the best grass grows. The animals are picketed only when there is danger from the Indians, or a prompt start is necessary.

A big fire is soon blazing; a part prepare the supper,—tea and coffee, bacon, trout, potatoes, good bread and butter, and, to-night, a grouse soup, the best use Governor Hunt can make of an old bird he shot on the road, to-day, and very good use it proved, too, by help of tin pail, potatoes and butter;—others feed the fire, bring the water, and prepare the camp for sleeping. An old canvass cloth serves for table; we squat on our blankets around it, and with tin cups, tin plates, knife and fork and spoon, take what is put before us, and are more than content. Eating rises to a spiritual enjoyment after such a day; and the Trois Freres or Delmonico does not offer a "squarer meal" than Governor Hunt. The "world's people" make their beds against a huge tree, and cut and plant boughs around the heads to keep out the cold wind; but the old campers drop their blankets anywhere around the fire; and after going back over the day and forward to the morrow in a pleasant chat, sitting around the glowing mass of flame and coal, we crawl in under our blankets, in a grand circle about the now smouldering logs, say our prayers to the twinkling stars up through the trees, and,—think of those new spring beds invented in Springfield!

We broke up housekeeping and started into the Park by nine o'clock the next morning. It isn't an easy matter to make an earlier start, when we have to carry our homes with us; cook and eat breakfast; wash the dishes; catch the animals; pack up beds and provisions; clean up camp, and reconstruct not only for a day's journey, but for a family moving. A short ride brought us into miles of clear prairie, with grass one to two feet high, and hearty streams struggling to be first into the Pacific Ocean. This was the Middle Park, and we had a long twenty-five miles ride northerly through it that day. It was not monotonous by any means. Frequent ranges of hills break the prairie; the latter changes from rich bottom lands with heavy grass, to light, cold gravelly uplands, thin with bunch grass and sage brush; sluggish streams and quick streams alternate; belts of hardy pines and tender looking aspens (cotton-wood) lie along the crests or sides of hills; farther away are higher hills fully wooded, and still beyond, "the range" that bounds the Park and circles it with eternal snows. The sun shines warm; there are wide reddish walls of granite or sandstone along many of the hills; some of the intervales are rich with green grass; and the sky is deep blue; and yet the prevailing tone and impression of the Park is a coldish gray. You find it on the earth; you see it in the subdued, tempered, or faded greens of leaf and shrub and grass; it hangs over the distant mountains; it prevails in the rocks; you feel it in the air,—a certain sort of stintedness or withholding impresses you, amid the magnificence of distance, of height and breadth and length, with which you are surrounded, and which is the first and greatest and most constant thought of the presence.

We scattered along wildly enough; some stopping to catch trout; others humoring lazy mules and horses; others to enjoy at leisure the novel surroundings,—meeting, with fellow-feeling, for lunch and the noon rest, but dividing again for the afternoon ride. All had gone before,—leaders, guides, packs, and were out of sight,—when my friend and especial companion on this trip, Mr. Hawkins of Mill City, of Springfield raising and relation, and myself rose over the hill that looked down into the valley that was our destination. It was a broad, fine vision. Right and left, several miles apart, ran miniature mountain ranges,— before, six miles away, rose an abrupt gray mountain wall; just beneath

Berthoud Pass at about the time of the Bowles expedition.

it, through green meadow, ran the Grand River;* up to us a smooth, clean, gradual ascent; along the river bank, a hundred white tents, like dots in the distance, showed the encampment of six to eight hundred Ute Indians, awaiting our party with "heap hungry" stomachs; in the upper farther corner, under the hill-side, a faint mist and steam in the air located the famous Hot Springs of the Middle Park,—the whole as complete a picture of broad, open plain, set in mountain frame, as one would dream of. It spurred our lagging spirits, and we galloped down the long plane, whose six miles seemed to the eye not a third so long in this dry, pure air.

Reaching the river, through the Indian encampment, whose mongrel curs alone gave fighting greeting, it looked deep and was boisterous;

---

*Now the Colorado River.

our animals hesitated; and we thought sympathetically of Bayard Taylor's sad fortune in making this hard journey into the Middle Park to see and try the Hot Springs, and then being obliged by the flood to content himself with a distant view from this bank of the river. But our comrades had gone over; and the only question was where. Looking for their track, directly there came galloping to our relief a gayly costumed Indian princess,—we were sure she was,—bare-backed for her haste to succor, and full of sweet sympathy for our anxiety, and tender smiles for our—attractiveness in misfortune. Plunging boldly into what seemed to us the deepest and swiftest part of the stream,—as doubtless it was,—she beckoned us to follow, with every enticing expression of eye and lips and hand; and follow we, of course, did,—had it been more dangerous we should,—and by folding ourselves up on the highest parts of our animals, we got through without serious wetting. But it proved that we crossed in the wrong place, and that our beautiful Indian princess, with beads and feathers and bright eyes and seductive ways, was only a plain young "buck,"—not even a maiden, not so much as a squaw, not, to come down to the worst at once, so near to glory and gallantry as a relationship to the Chief. Nothing less than the welcome we had from one of the best women of Colorado,—whom we parted from last in Fifth Avenue, and now found spending the summer with her family in a log cabin of one room, with eight hundred Indians for her only neighbors,—and the arrival of her husband from his afternoon's fishing with two bushels of fine trout packed over his horse's back,—here only was adequate soothing and consolation for our chagrin. And we didn't go into camp that night till after supper,—after supper of fresh biscuits, fried trout, and mountain raspberries!

Let me celebrate these high mountain raspberries before the taste goes from my mouth. They grow freely on the hill-sides, from seven thousand to ten thousand feet up, on bushes from six to eighteen inches high, are small and red, and the only wild fruit of the region worth eating. They are delicate and high-flavored to extreme; their mountain home refines and elevates them into the very concentration and essence of all frutiness; they not only tickle but intoxicate the palate,—so wild and aromatic, indeed, are they that they need some sugar to tone the flavor down to the despiritualized sense of a cultivated taste. Yet they are not so sour as to require sweetening,—only too high-toned for the stranger stomach; after sharing their native air a few days, we found them best picked and eaten from the vines. It is one of the motives

Grand Lake in Middle Park.

of family excursion parties into the mountains at this season to lay in
a supply of raspberry jam for the year; while the men catch trout, the
women pick raspberries, cook and sugar them in the camp-kettle, and
go home laden with this rare fruity sweetmeat. Here in the Middle Park
we were kept in full supply of the fresh fruit by the Ute squaws, who,
going off into the hills in the morning, often two together astride the
same pony, and a little papoose strapped on its board over the back
of one, would come back at night with cups and pails of the berries
to exchange with the whites for their own two great weaknesses, sugar
and biscuit. But the bears get the most of the raspberries so far. They
are at home with them during all the season, and can pick and eat at
leisure.

The Hot Springs of the Middle Park are both a curiosity and a virtue.
They are a considerable resort already by Coloradans at this season,
and when convenient roads are made over into the Park, there will be
a great flow of visitors to them. We found twenty or thirty other visitors here, scattered about in the neighborhood, while parties were coming and going every day. The springs for bathing, and the rivers for
fishing, are the two great attractions. On the hill-side, fifty feet above
the Grand River, and a dozen rods away, these hot sulphurous waters
bubble up at three or four different places within a few feet, and coming
together into one stream flow over an abrupt bank, say a dozen feet
high, into a little circular pool or basin below. Thence the waters scatter
off into the river. But the pool and the fall unite to make a charming
natural bathing-house. You are provided with a hot sitz bath and douche
together. The stream that pours over the precipice into the pool is about
as large as would flow out of a full water pail turned over, making a
stream three to five inches in diameter. The water is so hot that you
cannot at first bear your hand in it, being 110° Fahrenheit in temperature, and the blow of the falling water and its almost scalding heat send
the bather shrieking out on his first trial of them; but with light experi-
ments, first an arm, then a leg, and next a shoulder, he gradually gets
accustomed to both heat and fall, and can stand directly under the stream
without flinching, and then he has such a bath as he can find nowhere
else in the world. The invigorating effects are wonderful; there is no
lassitude, no chill from it, as is usually experienced after an ordinary
hot bath elsewhere; though the water be 110° warm, and the air 30°
to 40° cold, the shock of the fall is such a tonic, and the atmosphere
itself is so dry and inspiring, that no reaction, no unfavorable effects
are felt, even by feeble persons, in coming from one into the other.

The first thing in the morning, the last at night did we renew our trial of this hot douche bath during our brief stay in the neighborhood, and the old grew young and the young joyous and rampant from the experience. Wonderful cures are related as having been effected by these springs; the Indians resort to them a good deal, put their sick horses into them, and are loth to yield control of them to the whites; and in view of their probable future value, there has been a struggle among the latter for their ownership. They are now in the hands of Mr. Byers of the Rocky Mountain News at Denver, under a title that will probably defy all disputants. The waters look and taste precisely like those of the Sharon Sulphur Springs in New York. The difference is that these are hot, those cold. They have deposited sulphur, iron and soda in quantity all about their path, and these are their probable chief ingredients.

Over a little hill from the springs, by the side of the Grand River, – the hill, the stream, and a half mile between us and the Indian encampment, – we settled down in camp for two days and a half, studying Indian life, catching and eating trout, taking hot douche baths in the springs, and making excursions over the neighboring hills into side valleys. The river before us offered good fishing, but better was to be found in Williams Fork, a smaller stream a few miles below, where a half day's sport brought back from forty to sixty pounds of as fine speckled trout as ever came from brooks or lakes of New England. They ranged from a quarter of a pound up to two pounds weight each, and we had them at every meal.

The Indians were very neighborly; hill, stream and distance were no impediment to their attentions; their ponies would gallop with them over all in five minutes; and from two to a dozen, men and boys, never the squaws, were hanging about our camp fires from early morning till late evening. Curiosity, begging and good-fellowship were their only apparent motives; they did no mischief; they stole nothing, though food and clothing, pistols and knives, things they coveted and needed above all else, were loosely scattered about within reach; they only became a nuisance by being everlastingly in the way and spoiling the enjoyment of one's food by their wistful observation. Mrs. Browning says, you remember, that observation, which is not sympathy, is simply torture. And not a bit of sympathy did they show in our eating except as they shared. We were as liberal as our limited stores would allow; but the capacity of a single Indian's stomach is boundless; what could we do for the hundreds?

These Utes are a good deal higher grade of Indian than I had supposed. They are above the average of our Indian tribes in comeliness and intelligence; and none perhaps are better behaved or more amenable to direction from the whites. There are seven different bands or tribes of them, who occupy the mountains and parks of Colorado and adjoining sections of New Mexico and Utah. The bands number from five hundred to one thousand each. This one consisted of about seventy-five "lodges" or families, each represented by a tent of cloth stretched over a bunch of poles gathered at the top, and spreading around in a small circle. The poles leave a hole in the top for the smoke of a fire in the center beneath, and around which the family squat on their blankets and pile their stores of food and skins and clothing. Probably there were six hundred in the camp near us, men, women and children. They look frailer and feebler than you would expect; I did not see a single Indian who was six feet high or would weigh over one hundred and seventy-five pounds; they are all, indeed, under size, and no match in nervous or physical force for the average white man. Some of both sexes are of very comely appearance, with fine hands and delicate feet, and shapely limbs, with a bright mulatto complexion, and clear, piercing eyes; but their square heads, coarse hair, hideous daubs of yellow and red paint on the cheek and forehead, and motley raiment,—here a white man's cast-off hat, coat or pantaloons, if squaw a shabby old gown of calico or shirt of white cloth, alternate with Indian leggins and moccasins, bare legs and feet, a dirty white or flaming red blanket, beaded jacket of leather, feathers, and brass or tin trinkets hanging on the head, from the ears, down the back or breast,—all these disorderly and unaccustomed combinations give them at first a repulsive and finally a very absurd appearance. The squaws seem to be kept in the background, and, except when brides or the wives of a chief, dress much more plainly and shabbily than the bucks. They are all more modest and deferential in appearance and manners than would be expected; and I saw no evidence of or taste for strong drink among this tribe,—none of them ever asked for it, while their desire for food, especially for sugar and biscuit, was always manifest. The sugar they gobble up without qualification, and such unnatural food as this and fine flour breed diseases and weaknesses that are already destroying the race. Coughs are frequent, and dyspepsia; sickness and deaths are quite common among the children; and this incongruous mixture of white man's food and raiment and life with their own, which their contact with civilization has led them into, is sapping their vitality at its fountains. To make matters the worse, they have got hold of our quack medicines, and are great customers for Brandreth and other pills, with the vain hope of curing their maladies. In short, they are simple, savage children, and in that definition we find suggested the only proper way for the government to treat them.

Their wealth consists in their horses, which they breed or steal from their enemies of other tribes, and of which this tribe in the Middle Park must have a couple of hundred. They live on the game they can find in the parks and among the mountains, moving from one spot to another, as seasons and years change, the proceeds of the skins of the deer and other animals they kill, roots, nuts and berries, and the gifts of the government and the settlers. It is altogether even a precarious and hard reliance; the game is fast disappearing, — save of trout we have not seen enough in all our travels among the mountains to feed our small party upon, if it had all been caught; and the government agents are not always to be depended upon in making up deficiencies. Our neighbors had lately come over from the North Park, where they had hunted antelope to some purpose and with rare fortune, killing four thousand in all in two or three weeks, half of them in a single grand hunt. They cut the meat into thin slices and dry it, so that it looks like strips of old leather; and as we went about their camp we saw the little, weakly children pulling away at bits of it, apparently with not very satisfactory results. Our tribe was in trouble about a chief; the old one was dead, and there were two or three contestants for the succession; but the wrangle was not half so fierce as would arise over a contested election for mayor of a white man's city.

Affairs always seemed very quiet in the Indian camp in the daytime; the braves played cards, or did a little hunting; the squaws gathered wood, tanned skins, braided lariats, or made fantastic leather garments; the boys chased the ponies; but at night they as invariably appeared to be having a grand pow-wow, — rude music and loud shouting rolled up to our camp a volume of coarse sound that at first seemed frightful, as if the preparatory war-whoop for a grand scalping of their white neighbors, but which we learned to regard as the most innocent of barbaric amusements. Though these Utes are quite peaceful and even long-suffering towards the whites, they bear eternal enmity to the Indian tribes of the Plains, and are always ready to have a fight with them. Each party is strongest on its own territory, — the Arapahoes, Comanches and Cheyennes on the prairies, and the Utes among the hills; and each, while eager to receive the party of the other part at home, rarely go a-visiting. The Plains Indians are better mounted and better armed; chiefly because, keeping up nearly constant warfare with the whites, they have exacted prompter presents and larger pay from the government. The Utes complain, and with reason, that their friendliness causes them to be neglected and cheated; while their and our enemies thrive on government bounty.

There is now a plan for all the Ute tribes to go together into the south-western corner of Colorado, away from the mines and the whites, and there, upon abundant pastures and fruitful mountains, engage in a pastoral and half agricultural life; to set up stock-raising on a large scale, and such tillage as they can bring themselves to, under the protection and aid of the government. The scheme is a good one; the Indians agree to it; and the bargain has been made by the government agents here,—all that is needed is for the authorities at Washington to furnish the means for carrying it into execution. So far as our observation extends, the greatest trouble with our Indian matters lies at Washington; the chief of the cheating and stupidity gathers there; while the Indian agents here upon the ground are, if not immaculate, certainly more intelligent, sensible, and practical, and truer to the good of the settler and the Indian than their superiors at the seat of government.

Twin Lakes, Upper Arkansas Valley, September, 1868.

The circle of our Colorado and border travel experience has been made complete by an Indian scare. We have shared the horrible excitement of the settlers, when the hostile Indians put on their war-paint, raise their war-whoop, and dash wildly upon the life and property of the whites. Just as we were going into camp,—weary with mountain travel, and our heaviest teams far behind,—this side the range, there dashed in, on a gaunt white horse, a grim messenger from Denver, with official advices to Governor Hunt that the Indians of the Plains,—the Cheyennes, Arapahoes and Sioux,—were on the "war-path;" that from seeming friends they had suddenly turned again to open foes; and were raiding furiously all among the settlements, east, north and south of Denver, stealing horses and shooting the people. We were besought to keep among the mountains,—the homes of the friendly Utes,—as the only place of safety, for our company of territorial and federal officials would be a tempting prize for the red men; but the messenger, who proved

Twin Lakes.

to be a villainous sensationist, – though of course we did not know this then, – added to his written reports the alarming story that he had met the hostile Indians in the mountains, only that very day, that they had pursued and shot at him, – the rascal even showing as proof the bullet-holes in his saddle, – that he barely escaped by rapid riding, and that they were probably but a few miles back, and on our path.

Here was serious business, indeed, for such a party; burdened with overloaded wagons, tired horses and defenceless women and children; and all on pleasure and not on war intent. Messengers were sent back to hasten to camp all stragglers, and to warn the Indian agent, with his load of goods and rifles in the Park, to be on his guard, and to come forward. The secret could be kept from no one; the confusion and the excitement quickly grew intense; and that peculiar recklessness or indifference as to ordinary matters, that follows the presence of a deep emotion, was singularly manifest. Tents were shabbily put up; camp was disorderly made; supper was eaten in that mechanical, forced way, without regard to quantity, quality or clean plates, that happens when death is in the house; and elaborate toilets were dispensed with. But we huddled close in together; the animals were picketed near at hand; our fire-arms were put in good order; and up and down the road, trusty sentinels were posted. On each side were high abrupt hills; it was a "lovely spot" for an ambuscade; but the nearest anybody came to being killed was when one of our sentinels, during the midnight blackness of storm, suddenly entered upon the ground of the other. Indian-shod in sandals, and moving with that noiseless, stealthy tread that hunters unconsciously adopt, the one was almost upon the other before the latter discovered a foreign presence. There was a sudden click of the rifle's cock, a peremptory demand for "personal explanation" without delay, and then,—a friendly instead of a deadly greeting.

But it was a night to remember, with a shiver,—lying down in that far-off wilderness with the reasonable belief that before morning there was an even chance of an attack of hostile Indians upon our camp, more than half of whose numbers were women and children,—after an evening spent in discussing the tender ways Indians had with their captives, illustrated from the personal knowledge of many present; aroused after the first hour's feverish rest by a new messenger from another quarter, galloping into camp, and shouting, as if we were likely to forget, that "the Indians were loose, and hell was to pay;" followed by the coming of furious storm of rain and hail and thunder and lightning, sucking under our tents, beating through them, to wet pillows and blankets,— at any other time a dire grievance, now hardly an added trial; every ear stretched for unaccustomed sound, every heart beating anxiously, but every lip silent; all eagerly awaiting the slow-coming morning to bring renewal of life and the opportunity to go farther on and to safer retreats. To confess the unprosaic individual fact,—while I report the general truth,—this deponent had the soundest, sweetest night's sleep he had had in the mountains. Some natures will be perverse, and if one must be nervous, it is a great help to be conscious of it.

. . . The scare wore off under the tonic of a cool, clear morning, with splendid visions of fresh fields of snow glancing in the sunlight, the arrival of our load of rifles and Indian goods safe, a good breakfast of trout and Governor Hunt's best griddle-cakes, and the following summons to horse for the Twin Lakes. Never party moved out of camp more gladly; and a few miles farther on, the Arkansas valley welcomed us into a new country, full of the light and the freshness and the joy of a newly awakened nature. There was a California roll to the hills that led down to the river; the sage bush that covered them was greener and more stalwart than that of the Middle Park; and the river bottom held a deeper toned grass, and was alive with grazing cattle; while the Sahwatch range of mountains, that divides the Arkansas valley from the Pacific waters, was continuously higher than any we had yet looked up to, and its bold majestic peaks bore and brought far down their middles that thin new snow, which is such a touching type of purity, and is never seen without a real enthusiasm. Governor Bross and Vice-President Colfax, who had been off spending the night among the miners of an upper gulch, greeted us, too, with felicitations on our safety, and with a company of volunteer cavalry, that did not desert us until all apprehensions of danger had passed away.

Crossing the river, descending the valley, and then turning up among the western hills, over one, two lines of them, racing and roystering along with our new companions, and in our new joys, we suddenly came out over the Twin Lakes, and stopped. The scene was, indeed, enchanting. At our feet, a half a mile away, was the lower of two as fine sheets of water as mountain ever shadowed, or wind rippled, or sun illuminated. They took their places at once in the goodly company of the Cumberland Lakes of England, of Lucerne in Switzerland, of Como and Laggiore in north Italy, of Tahoe and Donner in California, and no second rank among them all. One is about three miles by a mile and a half; the other say two miles by one; and only a fifty-rod belt of grass and grove separates them. Above them on two sides sharply rise, — dark with trees and rocks until the snow caps with white, — the mountains of the range; sparsely-wooded hills of grass and sage brush mount gracefully in successive benches on a third, — it was over these that we came into their presence; while to the south a narrow, broken valley, pushed rapidly by the mountains towards the Arkansas, carries their outlet stream to its home in the main river. Clear, hard, sandy beaches alternate with walls of rock and low marshy meadows in making the immediate surroundings of both lakes. The waters are purity itself, and trout abound in them.

Here we camped for that and the next day, which was Sunday; restored our Indian-broken nerves; caught trout and picked raspberries; bathed in the lakes; rode up and around them; looked into their waters, and on over them to the mountains, — first green, then blue, then black, finally white, and then higher to clouds, as changing in color under storm, under sun, under moon, under lightning. Every variety of scene, every change and combination of cloud and color were offered us in these two days; and we worshipped, as it were, at the very fountains of beauty, where its every element in nature lay around, before, and above us.

Also, not to live forever in poetry, we patched our clothes, greased our boots, washed our handkerchiefs and towels,—one would dry while another was being washed, in the dry, breezy air,—and ate boiled onions and raspberry short-cake to repletion. Bayard Taylor's letters are at least a guide to the opportunities for good dinners in Colorado; and ostensibly with the purpose to explore the lakes, and see the falls in the river above, possibly with a thought to fall upon such hospitality as he experienced in the little neighboring village of Dalton,—another collection of vacant cabins, with a new court-house, and only two occupied tenements,—a few of us stole quietly off for a Sunday excursion.

We circled the lakes, as beautiful in detail as in grand effect; picked out many a charming camping-ground for future visits; found along the shores one or two resident families, and a tent with a stove-pipe through it, where a Chicago invalid was spending the summer, gaining vigorous strength and permanent health, and drying quantities of trout,—think of trout so plenty as to suggest drying them!—followed up the bed of the stream two miles or more above the lakes to a very pretty waterfall, and a deep pool, worn out of solid rock, thick with visible trout, whom we could poke with long sticks, but could not seduce with fattest of grasshoppers; lunched off the mountain raspberry vines; tracked a grizzly bear; and looked up the far-stretching gorge through rocks and bushes and vines that were very seducing,—but came back to Dalton in time to get our invitation to dinner. There was white table-cloth, and chairs, and fresh beefsteak, and mealy potatoes, and soft onions, and cream for coffee, and raspberry short-cake "to kill," and a lady and gentleman for hostess and host; everything and more and better even than Taylor had two years before. Going back by the lakes to camp just at sunset, they were in their best estate of color, of light and shade; and water and mountain and sky met and mingled, and led on the eye from one glory to another, till the joy of the spirit overcame and subdued and elevated the satisfaction of the senses.

HELEN HUNT JACKSON.

1878

In the late nineteenth century Colorado's arid climate and preponderance of cloudless days attracted a great number of people seeking relief from chronic respiratory ailments, and Colorado Springs in particular quickly gained a reputation for its sanitoria and specialization in the treatment of tuberculosis. Among the infirm who ventured to the Springs in 1873 was writer Helen Maria Fiske Hunt, known pseudonymously to her readers as "H.H.," "Saxe Holm," and even "Rip Van Winkle." She soon met a wealthy Colorado Springs businessman, William Shappless Jackson, and their subsequent marriage permitted her for the first time to write without the burden of deadlines or financial exigency.

Such flexibility may have made Helen Hunt Jackson one of the most influential writers of her day. After spending months at the Astor Library in New York City researching American Indian policy, she produced *A Century of Dishonor* (1881) and sent every member of Congress a copy at her own expense. The book was a scathing indictment of American policy toward the Red Man, and quickly earned its author the position of special commissioner on Indian affairs for the state of California. But to her bitter disappointment, the job turned out to be nothing more than a sinecure. Jackson's frustration produced another classic work on the mistreatment of Indians, the novel *Ramona* (1884). The book is best remembered not only for its depiction of the Indian problem in California, but also for its portrayal of Spanish-California aristocracy in decline.

On Colorado matters Jackson's writing was much less austere. Writing for such widely read magazines as *Scribner's* and *The Atlantic Monthly,* Jackson lauded the Colorado landscape in the kind of style that might have been expected of a woman writer of the Victorian era. She had a particular hankering for wildflowers, canyons ("No two canyons are alike to true lovers of canyons"), and the transitory nature of mining camps. While not the best example of the kind of "moral" journalism of which Jackson was capable, "Georgetown and the Terrible Mine" still brings to the reader a strong sense of Jackson's love for her adopted home.

GEORGETOWN AND THE TERRIBLE MINE

GEORGETOWN IS THE American cousin of Bad-Gastein. As Bad-Gastein crowds, nestles, wedges itself into a valley among the Austrian Alps, so does Georgetown crowd, nestle, wedge itself into its canyon among the Rocky Mountains. And as the River Ach runs through and in the streets of Gastein, so runs Clear Creek in and through the streets of Georgetown. But Clear Creek does not leap, like the Ach. Georgetown has no waterfall. Neither are the sides of the canyon wooded, like the beautiful, glittering sides of the Gastein Valley. Georgetown is bare and brown. Georgetown is Gastein stripped of its fortune, come to the New World to begin anew in the hard pioneer life. In the old days of Gastein, silver and gold mines were worked in all the mountains round about. Those were the days of the haughty Weitmosers, whose history is wrought into legends, and linked with every rock and forest and waterfall in the Gastein Valley. Now the Weitmoser name is seen only on tombstones, and the water-wheels and sluices of the old gold mines are slowly rotting away. Perhaps three hundred years hence the steep sides of the Georgetown Canyon will be covered again with balsams and pines; the pinks, daisies, and vetches will carpet the ground as the pink heath does in Gastein; the mill-wheels will stand still; the mines will be empty; and pilgrims will seek the heights as they seek Gastein's, not because they hold silver and gold, but because they are gracious and beautiful and health-giving.

To Georgetown, as to Gastein, there is but one easy way of going,— that is, by private carriage. The public coaches are here, as everywhere, uncomfortable, overloaded, inexorable. I know of no surer way to rob a journey of all its finest pleasures, than to commit one's self to one of these vehicles. It means being obliged to get up at hours you abhor, to sit close to people you dislike, to eat when you are not hungry, to go slowest when there is nothing to see and fastest when you would gladly linger for hours, to be drenched with rain, choked with dust, and never have a chance to pick a flower. It means misery.

The private carriage, on the other hand, means so much of delight, freedom, possession, that it is for ever a marvel to me that all travellers with money, even with a little money, do not journey in that way. Good horses, an open carriage, bright skies overhead; beloved faces,— eager, responsive, sympathetic,—on either hand; constant and an unrestrained interchange of thought, impression, impulse,—all this, and the glorious out-door world added! Is there a way of being happier? I think not.

It was thus that we set out, early on a June day, to go from Central City to Georgetown.

"Up to Georgetown," somebody said in our hearing.

"Is there any going further up?" we exclaimed.

It had not seemed that there could be. Did not the sky rest on the tops of the sharp-precipiced hills near whose summits we were clinging?

Nevertheless it was "up" to Georgetown at first,—up through Nevada Gulch, a steeper, narrower, stonier, dirtier gulch than we had yet seen, more riddled with mines and crowded with more toppling houses. Then, out upon what seemed an "open" by comparison with the gulches, but was really only an interval of lesser hills and canyons. Deserted mills, mines, and cabins were here; hardly a trace of cultivation, but everywhere green shrubs and luxuriant flowers, to show what fertility was lying neglected in the unused soil. Three miles of this, and then, turning to the left, we plunged into a road so stony, so overgrown, it seemed hardly possible it could be the one we had been told to take to reach the top of Bellevue Mountain.

Let no one forget, in going from Central City to Georgetown, to ask for and find this wild path. Its outlook is worth all the rest of the journey.

It was a severe climb,—we did not know how severe, for our eyes were feasting on the wayside lovelinesses of green oak and juniper and golden asters, white daisies and purple vetches. From the bare and stony gulches we had left behind, to this fragrance and color, was a leap from a desert into a garden. Suddenly looking up, we found that we were also looking off. We were on a grand ridge or divide, around which seemed to centre semicircles of mountains. So high and so separated is this ridge, and yet so central in the great fields of peaks which make up this part of the great Rocky Mountain chain, that, while we could look off far enough to see the Snowy Range, we could also look down into the canyons and gorges among the nearer mountains. It was a surpassing sight! It is one of the few extended views I have seen which have also composition, beauty of grouping, and tenderness of significance and revelation. We could see long, shining, serrated spaces of the solid, snow-covered peaks, the highest on the continent,—peaks from whose summit one could look, if human vision were keen enough, to the Western and the Eastern Oceans. These lofty serrated lengths of shining snow lay cut against the uttermost horizon blue, like an alabaster wall rounding the very world. Seeming to join this wall, and almost in lines of concentric curves, were myriads and masses of lower mountains, more than the eye could count. To the very foot of the watch-tower ridge on which we stood, the peaks seemed crowded. We could look into the green valleys lying between them, and trace the brown thread of road winding up each valley. We sat under the shade of pines and firs. The ground was gay with yellow lupines, daisies, and great mats of killikinnick vines (the bear-berry) with full clusters of delicate pink bells, as lovely as arbutus blossoms, and almost as fragrant.

Ten thousand feet above the sea, and yet the air was as spicy and summer-laden as in an Italian June! Ten thousand feet above the sea, and yet the warm wind burnt our faces fiercely, and the snow-topped horizon wall seemed like a miracle under such a tropical sun!

On the very summit of the mountain, even here among the daisies and lupines, and within sight of all the solemn kingdoms of mountains, we came upon one who dug for gold. He was a German, tall, broad-chested, straight-shouldered, blue-eyed, flaxen-haired,—a superbly made man. Health and power actually seemed to radiate from him under the sunlight, and the unconscious joyousness of their unconscious possession lighted his eye and beamed in his smile. He stood all day long at the mouth of a shaft, and drew up buckets full of ore which might mean a few dollars of gold. It was an old claim. He had two partners in the ownership of it, and they were now working it for a few months, merely to comply with the provisions of the recent Miner's Act. He spoke that delicious and effective broken English which only Germans use. To him the Act meant personal inconvenience; but he had thought deeper than that. "It is good for the country. There will be not the wild cat any more. It shall be that a man do not throw his money away that another man shall move his stakes in the night."

I do not know why this man's figure seemed to me more typical of the true genius and soul of gold-winning than all the toiling crowds in mining towns. It was, perhaps, the loneliness of the spot, the glorious lift of it above the world around, or even the beauty of the blossoms and the scent of the firs. It might have been just such a nook in the Hartz Mountains to which the genii of gold and silver led the favored mortals to whom they elected to open the doors of their treasure-house.

From Bellevue Mountain to Idaho it is three miles, downhill. Not downhill in the ordinary acceptation of the word, not such downhill as one may have three miles of any day in northern New England; but downhill in a canyon,—that is, downhill between two other hills so sharp that they wall the road. Truly, labyrinths of interlacing hills can be marvellous. Much I question whether the earth holds anywhere a more delightful confusion than has been wrought out of these upheavals of the Rocky Mountains, and planted with firs and bluebells. In a hollow made by the mouth of the canyon down which we had driven, and by the mouths of several other canyons, all sharp-walled and many-curved, lay Idaho. From the tops of the mountains which circle it, the little handful of houses must look like a handful of pebbles at the bottom of an emerald-sided well. Thither come every summer multitudes of men and women, Coloradoans, Californians, and travellers from the East,—seeking to be made well and strong by bathing in hot soda springs, which bubble out of the rocks of a small creek.

For the benefit of those who, not being disciples of Hahnemann, do not shudder at the thought of medicated baths, I give the analysis of the water:—

Carbonate of Soda 30.80
Carbonate of Lime 9.52
Carbonate of Magnesia 2.88
Carbonate of Iron 4.12
Sulphate of Soda 29.36
Sulphate of Magnesia 18.72
Sulphate of Lime 3.44
Chloride of Sodium 4.16
Silicate of Soda 4.08
Chloride of Calcium and Magnesium, of each a trace.
                                                        _____
                                                        107.00

If it were proposed to any man to go into an apothecary's shop and take from the big jars on the shelves all these carbonates, sulphates, silicates, and chlorides, dissolve them in his bath-tub, and then proceed to soak himself in the water, absorbing the drugs through his million-pored skin, he would probably see the absurdity and the risk of the process. But, because Nature, for some mysterious purposes, has seen fit to brew these concoctions in the bowels of the earth, which spits them out as fast as it can, men jump at the conclusion that they are meant for healing purposes, and that one cannot drink too much of them, or stay in them too long.

"Do you take the baths yourself?" I asked the man in charge of the "Pioneer Bathing Establishment."

"Yes'm, I'm tryin' 'em. But if I stay in more'n fifteen minutes, I get just as weak as any thing,—real weak feeling all over; it seems as if I couldn't get out. But there's plenty of folks that comes and stays in an hour and a half, and say it does 'em good."

Nineteenth-century bird's-eye view of Georgetown.

"But are you not afraid of any thing which is so powerful that it makes you feel so weak in so few minutes? Why do you take the baths at all? Are you ill?" I said.

"No'm, I ain't sick. Leastways, nothing to speak of. I hain't ever been very strong. But I thought I'd try 'em. The doctors all say they're good, and I expect they must be; they ought to know. And I'm here all day, with not much of any thing to do. I might as well go in."

What an epitome of truth in the bathman's words! What an unconscious analysis of the process by which patients are made, — lack of occupation, and an ignorant faith in doctor's assertions.

Up a westward canyon from Idaho lies the road to Georgetown, — twelve miles of it. There is just room for it and for Clear Creek, and for narrow rims of cottonwood, willows, and wild roses, and for here and there a bit of farm. The sides of the canyon are sometimes bare, stony; sometimes green with pines and firs and young aspens; sometimes gray, because fire has killed the pines; sometimes gray with piles of ore thrown up from mouths of mines; always a changing succession of color; always a changing succession of shape, of contour. Ah! the twelve miles it is to remember; and alas! the twelve miles it is to long and yet fail to describe. Canyons after canyons open and shut as we pass. Just such a road as we are on flings its alluring brown thread up each one. If there were no such thing as a fixed purpose, and an inexorable appointed day, we would follow each clew and learn each canyon by heart. No two canyons are alike to true lovers of canyons, any more than any two faces are alike to the student of faces. To the outer edge of the concentric, curving ranges of this Rocky Mountain chain one might journey, in and out and up and over, and in and out and in and out again, I am persuaded, all summer long, for summers and summers, and find no monotony, no repetition. That is, if one be a lover; and if one be not, what use in being alive? Rather, one should say, in having a name to live while one is dead.

Georgetown is a surprise at last. It has no straggling outposts of houses, and you have become so absorbed in climbing the canyon, watching the creek and the mountains, the trees and the flowers, that you forget that a town is to come. Suddenly you see it full in view, not many rods ahead, wedged, as I said before, like Bad-Gastein, — crowded, piled, choked in at the end of the narrowed rift up which you have climbed. In and out among the narrow streets runs the creek, giving shining and inexplicable glimpses of water, here, there, and everywhere, among the chimney-tops and next to doorsteps. The houses are neat, comfortable, and have a suggestion of home-loving and abiding, quite unlike the untamed and nomadic look of Central City. You turn corner after corner, crossing the mountain side sharply at each turn, and getting up higher and higher, street by street, till on the very highest level you come to the Barton House, and look off from its piazza over the roofs of the town. On either hand are towering mountain sides, dotted wellnigh to the tops with the shining pyramids of the gray ore thrown up by mines. They mark lines like ledges hundreds of feet above the town. The hills are honey-combed by galleries and shafts; but they look still and peaceful and sunny as the virgin hills of the Tyrol.

"Shall we go down into a silver mine? Have you had enough of mines?" said the one experienced in mines.

"Never enough of mines," I replied. "And down into a mine must be a thing quite unlike headforemost into a mine. Let us go."

"Then I will take you to the 'Terrible Mine,' " he said. "It is the nearest and one of the largest."

"Is it so very terrible?" I asked. The word was not alluring.

"Only 'Terrible' by reason of the amount of money sunk in it," he laughed. "It is the most picturesquely situated and attractive mine I know of. But it has swallowed up more money than any other three mines in the region, and is only just now beginning to pay."

As the horses' heads were turned sharp to the right from the hotel door and we began to climb again, I exclaimed, incredulously: "What, still further up?"

"Oh, yes! two miles straight up. There might be a ladder set from here to there if one could be made long enough," was the reply. If it had been a ladder it would have seemed safer. A narrow shelf on the precipitous side of the mountain,—winding, zigzagging up in a series of sharp curves, with only a slight banking of the earth and the stone at the outer edge, and a sheer wall hundreds of feet below, down to the foaming creek,—this is the terrible road up to the "Terrible Mine." It was like swinging out into space when we turned the corners. Teams heavily loaded with silver ore were coming down. In places where two inches' room made all the odds between being dashed over the precipice and not, we passed them,—that is, our carriage passed them. We were not in it. We were standing close to the inner wall, backed up against it, holding our breaths to make ourselves thin. "Can't go on the outside, sir, with this load," was the firm though respectfully sympathizing reply of teamster after teamster; and on the outer and almost crumbling edge of the road, where the heavy load of ore would have been in danger of crushing down the entire shelf, there our wheels were airily poised, waiting for the wagons to pass. More than once, watching closely from behind, I failed to see even a rim of road beyond the wheel. One careless misstep of a horse, one instant's refusal to obey the rein, and the carriage would have topped over and down into the foam. Yet our driver seemed as unconcerned as if he had been driving on a broad boulevard, and had evidently a profound contempt for his passengers, who persisted in jumping from the carriage at every turn-out.

The creek was one pauseless torrent of white foam. All the beautiful amber spaces were gone. Not a breath did it take; it seemed like two miles of continuous waterfall. Tall fir-trees shaded it, but their tops were far below us; their shining darkness made the white of the foaming water all the whiter by contrast. On the rocky wall on our right were waving flowers and shrubs,—columbines, bluebells, spiraeas; so slight their hold they seemed but to have just alighted, like gay-winged creatures, who might presently soar and pass on.

One thread-like stream of water came down this precipice. It zigzagged to get down as much as we were zigzagging to get up. At turn after turn in the road we continued to see new leaps, new falls of it, until at last we saw the spot where it cleft the uppermost rock, looking like nothing but a narrow, fleecy wisp of cloud, lying half on the gray summit and half on the blue sky.

The miners' cabins were perched here and there among the bowlders, hundreds of feet up, bare, shelterless, remote. They looked more like homes for eagles than for men. No path led to them; no green thing, save firs and low oaks, grew near them; only by the sharp roof-tree line could one tell them from the rocks which were piled around them.

At the end of two miles, we came to a spot where creek and road and precipice paused and widened. The creek was dammed up, making a smooth, clear lake, with odd little pine-planked bridge-paths circling it; the road space widened into a sheltered, shady spot, where, nestled against the mountain of stone, stood three or four small buildings. A fountain played before one and children played before the others. These were the offices and homes of the men in charge of the mine, and the mouth of the mine was in sight, high up on the mountain side. An enormous pyramid of the glistening gray ore lay in front of it. On the top of this two men were at work loading the ore into small buckets, swung on wire from the mouth of the mine to the top of a high derrick on the edge of the creek. Back and forth and back and forth glided the buckets, swift and noiseless. The wire was but just visible in the air; the buckets seemed, coming and going, like huge shining shuttles, flung by invisible hands.

By gasps we threaded our way among the bowlders and up to the mouth of the mine. Here, indeed, a ladder would have been a help.

Then, miners' jackets on our shoulders, candles in our hands, facing an icy wind and breathing the fumes of gunpowder, again we entered the earth by an oven-door in a rock. We walked on the iron rails of the track, down which cars loaded with ore came constantly rumbling out of the darkness. We shrank into crannies of the rock to let them pass. The track was wet and slippery. It seemed a long way, but was only a few hundred feet, before we came to a vaulted chamber, so dimly lighted that it looked vast. Strange sounds came from its centre. As our eyes gradually grew used to the darkness, a strange shape in its centre grew gradually distinct. The sounds and the shape were one. It was a steam-engine. It was at work. Puff, puff, hiss, creak, slide,—weird beyond all power of words to say sounded these noises in that ghostly place. A gnome-like shape, in semblance of a man, stood by, with a controlling hand on the puffing engine.

"Would you like to go down in the mine?" said the Shape, courteously.

It was a hospitable gnome. This was the one entertainment at his command. Tremblingly I said "Yes." The Shape disappeared. We were left alone in the vaulted chamber. The steam-engine stopped. No sound broke the silence. The darkness seemed to grow darker. I reached out for a friendly hand, and was just about to say, "This is, indeed, the 'Terrible Mine,'" when a sudden light flashed into the place, and springing back, I saw the head of another Shape coming up from an aperture at my feet. A trap-door had been flung open. The Shape had a lighted candle in the band of his cap. If I were to describe him as he appeared to me in that first instant, I should say that frightful flames issued from his forehead. He smiled friendlily; but I grasped the protecting hand closer.

"Is the lady coming down, sir? The bucket will be up in a minute," he said.

This was the mouth of the shaft. The Shape had crawled up on a ladder. It was no more than an ordinary front stairs to him.

Bottom of the shaft.

I was ashamed to say how afraid I grew. The Shape answered my unspoken thought.

"There's ladies goes down every day. There's no danger,—not the least," he said.

"Ye wouldn't miss it, not for any thing."

The bucket came up. It was swung off to one side of the trap-door. It was an extra-sized water-pail, with high sides,—sides coming up just above the knees of them who stood in it. It could hold just two,—no more. It was necessary to stand facing in a particular way to prevent its swinging round and round. By an iron hook from the centre of the handle it was suspended over the dark aperture. It was raised and lowered by the steam-engine.

"Ready?" said the Shape who stood with his hand on the engine.

"All ready," replied the Shape who stood with one hand on the edge of our bucket.

"Now, keep cool. Don't mind the bucket's swinging. The shaft ain't straight, and it will twist some. I'll be down there before you are. He'll let you down slow." And the friendly Shape vanished in the gloom.

It was odd how much it felt like being lowered by the hair of one's head, the going down in that bucket. It is odd how very little consciousness one has of any thing solid under one's feet, standing in such buckets under such circumstances. It is odder still what a comfort there is in a bit of lighted candle in this sort of place. All that the candle showed me was the slanting wooden wall, against which we bumped with great force every now and then. Why the sight of this should have been reassuring it is impossible to tell; but, during the hour—three minutes long—which we passed in that descending, swinging, twisting, bumping bucket I fixed my eyes on that candle-flame as earnestly as if it had been a lighthouse, and I a sailor steering to shore by its guidance.

"All right, ma'am. You didn't mind it much, did you?" came suddenly from the darkness, and a pair of strong hands laid violent hold on the bucket edge, and, resting it firm on a wet and stony ground, helped us out. This was the nethermost gallery of the mine. We were five hundred feet down in the earth and there were five galleries above our heads. We followed the friendly Shape over rocks, piles of ore, past mouths of pits, and through dripping water, to the end of the gallery, where we found a party of miners drilling and picking. Here and there we saw long, glistening veins of the precious ore in the walls over head. It seemed to run capriciously, branching now to right, now to left. Here and there we came to dark openings in the walls, through which our guide would call to men at work above us. Their voices reverberated in the heavy gloom and sounded preternaturally loud.

The place grew more and more weird and awesome at every step. The faces of the miners we met seemed to grow more and more unhuman, less and less friendly. I was glad when we began to retrace our steps; and the bucket, swinging in mid-air, looked like a welcome escape, a comforting link between us and the outer world. Whether bucket, shaft, steam-engine, or we were in fault I do not know; but the upward journey was a terrible one. The bucket swung violently,— almost round and round; our clothes had not been carefully secured, and they were caught between the bucket and the shaft-sides and wrenched and twisted; and, to add to the horror, our candle went out. No words were spoken in that bucket during those minutes; they were minutes not to be forgotten. Still the guide was right: we would not "have missed it for any thing."

When we offered our guide money, he said: "No, thank you. I don't take any money for myself; but, if you'll read that notice,"—pointing to a written paper on the office wall,—"perhaps you'll give us something for our reading-room." This paper stated that the miners were trying to collect money enough to build a small room, where they might have books and papers and perhaps now and then a lecture. They had subscribed among themselves nearly three hundred dollars.

"You see," said our guide, "if we had some such place as that, then the boys wouldn't go down to the town evenings and Sundays and get drunk. When a fellow's worked in a mine all day he's got to have something."

How the thought struck home to our hearts at that minute. We had been in that airless, sunless cavern only one short half hour; yet the blue sky, the light, the breeze, the space already seemed to us unreal. We were dazzled, bewildered. What must be the effect of weeks and months and years of such life?

"Indeed, we will give you all the help we can," we said; "and, what is more, we will ask everybody we know to send you some papers or books."

Here is the guide's address:

HENRY F. LAMPSHIRE,
Foreman of the "Terrible Mine,"
Georgetown,
Colorado.

From Georgetown down to Idaho at sunset is more beautiful even than from Idaho up to Georgetown of a morning.

Full speed; sunlight gone from the left-hand wall, broad gold bands of it on the right; now and then a rift or canyon opening suddenly to the west and letting in a full flood of light, making it sunny in a second, afternoon, when the second before it had been wellnigh sombre twilight and the second after it will be sombre twilight again; red, gray, and white clouds settling down in fleecy masses upon the snowy mountain towers of the gateway of the valley,—this is sunset between Georgetown and Idaho. And to us there came also a wayside greeting more beautiful than the clouds, bluer than the sky, and gladder than the sun,—only a flower, one flower! But it was the Rocky Mountain columbine,—peerless among columbines, wondrous among flowers. Waving at the top of a stem two feet high, surrounded by buds full two inches and a half in diameter, the inner petals stainless white, the outer ones brilliant blue, a sheaf of golden-anthered stamens in the centre,—there it stood, pure, joyous, stately, regal. We gazed in speechless delight into its face. There was a certain solemnity in its beauty.

"That's the gladdest flower I ever saw," were the first words spoken, and the face of the man who said them glowed.

Oh! wondrous power of a fragile thing, born for a single day of a single summer! I think that the thing I shall longest remember and always most vividly see of that whole trip in the Colorado canyons will be that fearless, stainless, joyful, regnant blossom, and my friend's tribute of look, of tone, when he said, "The gladdest flower I ever saw."

WALT WHITMAN.

1879

In 1845 a venturesome young newspaper editor from Brooklyn sent the people of the United States the following message:

> Stretching between the Allegheny Mountains and the Pacific Ocean, are millions on millions of uncultivated acres of land. . . . We have lofty views of the scope and destiny of the American Republic. It is for the interest of mankind that its power and territory should be extended. We claim those lands* thus, by a law superior to parchments and dry diplomatic rules. . . ."[3]

That was, as Bernard DeVoto characterized it much later, "the barbaric if adolescent yawp of Mr. Walter, as he still signed it, Whitman"[4] speaking to the nation from the pages of the Brooklyn *Eagle*.

Yet for all his haranguing on behalf of westward expansion, the author of *Leaves of Grass* did not travel to the Rocky Mountains until he was in his sixtieth year. Five years after suffering a paralytic stroke, "the good grey poet" was nonetheless the same youthful Whitman whose salvos extolling the virtues of American geography, democracy and patriotic sentiments had been launched from the offices of the *Eagle* thirty-four years before. Whitman had created a lifetime of expectations about the mountain West, and there is little reason to believe from the account that follows that he was disappointed in what he found when he visited Colorado in 1879.

---

*Whitman was referring to the lands then claimed by Mexico, which included about one-third of Colorado. These lands were ceded to the United States in 1848.

AERIAL EFFECTS

THE JAUNT OF FIVE OR six hundred miles from Topeka to Denver took me through a variety of country, but all unmistakably prolific, western, American, and on the largest scale. For a long distance we follow the line of the Kansas river, (I like better the old name, Kaw,) a stretch of very rich, dark soil, famed for its wheat, and call'd the Golden Belt—then plains and plains, hour after hour—Ellsworth county, the centre of the State— where I must stop a moment to tell a characteristic story of early days— scene the very spot where I am passing—time 1868. In a scrimmage at some public gathering in the town, A. had shot B., quite badly, but had not kill'd him. The sober men of Ellsworth conferr'd with one another and decided that A. deserv'd punishment. As they wished to set a good example and establish their reputation the reverse of a Lynch- ing town, they open an informal court and bring both men before them for deliberate trial. Soon as this trial begins the wounded man is led forward to give his testimony. Seeing his enemy in durance and unarm'd, B. walks suddenly up in a fury and shoots A. through the head—shoots him dead. The court is instantly adjourn'd, and its unanimous mem- bers, without a word of debate, walk the murderer B. out, wounded as he is, and hang him.

In due time we reach Denver, which city I fall in love with from the first, and have that feeling confirm'd, the longer I stay there. One of my pleasantest days was a jaunt, via Platte cañon, to Leadville.

AN HOUR ON KENOSHA SUMMIT.

Jottings from the Rocky Mountains, mostly pencill'd during a day's trip over the South Park RR., returning from Leadville, and especially the hour we were detain'd, (much to my satisfaction,) at Kenosha summit. As afternoon advances, novelties, far-reaching splendors, accumulate under the bright sun in this pure air. But I had better commence with the day.

The confronting of Platte cañon just at dawn, after a ten miles' ride in early darkness on the rail from Denver—the seasonable stoppage at the entrance of the cañon, and good breakfast of eggs, trout, and nice griddle-cakes—then as we travel on, and get well in the gorge, all the wonders, beauty, savage power of the scene—the wild stream of water, from sources of snows, brawling continually in sight one side—the dazzling sun, and the morning lights on the rocks—such turns and grades in the track, squirming around corners, or up and down hills—far glimpses of a hundred peaks, titanic necklaces, stretching north and south—the huge rightly-named Dome-rock—and as we dash along, others similar, simple, monolithic, elephantine.

AN EGOTISTICAL "FIND."

"I have found the law of my own poems," was the unspoken but more-and-more decided feeling that came to me as I pass'd, hour after hour, amid all this grim yet joyous elemental abandon—this plenitude of material, entire absence of art, untrammel'd play of primitive Nature—the chasm, the gorge, the crystal mountain stream, repeated scores, hundreds of miles the broad handling and absolute uncrampedness—the fantastic forms, bathed in transparent browns, faint reds and grays, towering sometimes a thousand, sometimes two or three thousand feet high—at their tops now and then huge masses pois'd, and mixing with the clouds, with only their outlines, hazed in misty lilac, visible. ("In Nature's grandest shows," says an old Dutch writer, an ecclesiastic, "amid the ocean's depth, if so might be, or countless worlds rolling above at night, a man thinks of them, weighs all, not for themselves or the abstract, but with reference to his own personality, and how they may affect him or color his destinies.")

NEW SENSES—NEW JOYS.

We follow the stream of amber and bronze brawling along its bed, with its frequent cascades and snow-white foam. Through the cañon we fly—mountains not only each side, but seemingly, till we get near, right in front of us—every rood a new view flashing, and each flash defying description—on the almost perpendicular sides, clinging pines, cedars, spruces, crimson sumach bushes, spots of wild grass—but dominating all, those towering rocks, rocks, rocks, bathed in delicate varicolors, with the clear sky of autumn overhead. New senses, new joys, seem develop'd. Talk as you like, a typical Rocky Mountain cañon, or a limitless sea-like stretch of the great Kansas or Colorado plains, under favoring circumstances, tallies, perhaps expresses, certainly awakes, those grandest and subtlest element-emotions in the human soul, that all the marble temples and sculptures from Phidias to Thorwaldsen—all paintings, poems, reminiscences, or even music, probably never can.

STEAM-POWER, TELEGRAPHS, &c.

I get out on a ten minutes' stoppage at Deer creek, to enjoy the unequal'd combination of hill, stone and wood. As we speed again, the yellow granite in the sunshine, with natural spires, minarets, castellated perches far aloft—then long stretches of straight-upright palisades, rhinoceros color—then gamboge and tinted chromos. Ever the best of my pleasures the cool-fresh Colorado atmosphere, yet sufficiently warm. Signs of man's restless advent and pioneerage, hard as Nature's face is— deserted dug-outs by dozens in the side-hills—the scantling-hut, the telegraph-pole, the smoke of some impromptu chimney or outdoor fire— at intervals little settlements of log-houses, or parties of surveyors or telegraph builders, with their comfortable tents. Once, a canvas office where you could send a message by electricity anywhere around the world! Yes, pronounc'd signs of the man of latest dates, dauntlessly grappling with these grisliest shows of the old kosmos. At several places steam saw-mills, with their piles of logs and boards, and the pipes puffing. Occasionally Platte cañon expanding into a grassy flat of a few acres. At one such place, toward the end, where we stop, and I get out to stretch my legs, as I look skyward, or rather mountain-topward, a huge hawk or eagle (a rare sight here) is idly soaring, balancing along the ether, now sinking low and coming quite near, and then up again in stately-languid circles—then higher, higher, slanting to the north, and gradually out of sight.

AMERICA'S BACK-BONE.

I jot these lines literally at Kenosha summit, where we return, after-noon, and take a long rest, 10,000 feet above sea-level. At this immense height the South Park stretches fifty miles before me. Mountainous chains and peaks in every variety of perspective, every hue of vista, fringe the view, in nearer, or middle, or far-dim distance, or fade on the horizon. We have now reach'd, penetrated the Rockies, (Hayden calls it the Front Range,) for a hundred miles or so; and though these chains spread away in every direction, specially north and south, thou-sands and thousands farther, I have seen specimens of the utmost of them, and know henceforth at least what they are, and what they look like. Not themselves alone, for they typify stretches and areas of half the globe—are, in fact, the vertebrae or back-bone of our hemisphere. As the anatomists say a man is only a spine, topp'd, footed, breasted and radiated, so the whole Western world is, in a sense, but an expan-sion of these mountains. In South America they are the Andes, in Central America and Mexico the Cordilleras, and in our States they go under different names—in California the Coast and Cascade ranges—thence more eastwardly the Sierra Nevadas—but mainly and more centrally here the Rocky Mountains proper, with many an elevation such as Lincoln's, Grey's, Harvard's, Yale's, Longs' and Pike's peaks, all over 14,000 feet high. (East, the highest peaks of the Alleghanies, the Adi-rondacks, the Cattskills, and the White Mountains, range from 2000 to 5500 feet—only Mount Washington, in the latter, 6300 feet.)

THE PARKS.

In the midst of all here, lie such beautiful contrasts as the sunken basins of the North, Middle, and South Parks, (the latter I am now on one side of, and overlooking,) each the size of a large, level, almost quadrangular, grassy, western county, wall'd in by walls of hills, and each park the source of a river. The ones I specify are the largest in Colorado, but the whole of that State, and of Wyoming, Utah, Nevada and western California, through their sierras and ravines, are copiously mark'd by similar spreads and openings, many of the small ones of paradisiac loveliness and perfection, with their offsets of mountains, streams, atmosphere and hues beyond compare.

ART FEATURES.

Talk, I say again, of going to Europe, of visiting the ruins of feudal castles, or Coliseum remains, or kings' palaces—when you can come *here*. The alternations one gets, too; after the Illinois and Kansas prairies of a thousand miles—smooth and easy areas of the corn and wheat of ten million democratic farms in the future—here start up in every conceivable presentation of shape, these non-utilitarian piles, coping the skies, emanating a beauty, terror, power, more than Dante or Angelo ever knew. Yes, I think the chyle of not only poetry and painting, but oratory, and even the metaphysics and music fit for the New World, before being finally assimilated, need first and feeding visits here.

Mountain streams.—The spiritual contrast and etheriality of the whole region consist largely to me in its never-absent peculiar streams—the snows of inaccessible upper areas melting and running down through the gorges continually. Nothing like the water of pastoral plains, or creeks with wooded banks and turf, or anything of the kind elsewhere. The shapes that element takes in the shows of the globe cannot be fully understood by an artist until he has studied these unique rivulets.

Aerial effects.—But perhaps as I gaze around me the rarest sight of all is in atmospheric hues. The prairies—as I cross'd them in my journey hither—and these mountains and parks, seem to be to afford new lights and shades. Everywhere the aerial gradations and sky-effects inimitable; nowhere else such perspectives, such transparent lilacs and grays. I can conceive of some superior landscape painter, some fine colorist, after sketching awhile out here, discarding all his previous work, delightful to stock exhibition amateurs, as muddy, raw and artificial. Near one's eye ranges an infinite variety; high up, the bare whitey-brown, above timber line; in certain spots afar patches of snow any time of year; (no trees, no flowers, no birds, at those chilling altitudes.) As I write I see the Snowy Range through the blue mist, beautiful and far off. I plainly see the patches of snow.

DENVER IMPRESSIONS.

Through the long-lingering half-light of the most superb of evenings we return'd to Denver, where I staid several days leisurely exploring, receiving impressions, with which I may as well taper off this memorandum, itemizing what I saw there. The best was the men, three-fourths of them large, able, calm, alert, American. And cash! why they create it here. Out in the smelting works, (the biggest and most improv'd ones, for the precious metals, in the world,) I saw long rows of vats, pans, cover'd by bubbling-boiling water, and fill'd with pure silver, four or five inches thick, many thousand dollars' worth in a pan. The foreman who was showing me shovel'd it carelessly up with a little wooden shovel, as one might toss beans. Then large silver bricks, worth $2000 a brick, dozens of piles, twenty in a pile. In one place in the mountains, at a mining camp, I had a few days before seen rough bullion on the ground in the open air, like the confectioner's pyramids at some swell dinner in New York. (Such a sweet morsel to roll over with a poor author's pen and ink—and appropriate to slip in here—that the silver product of Colorado and Utah, with the gold product of California, New Mexico, Nevada and Dakota, foots up an addition to the world's coin of considerably over a hundred millions every year.)

A city, this Denver, well-laid out—Laramie street, and 15th and 16th and Champa streets, with others, particularly fine—some with tall store-houses of stone or iron, and windows of plate-glass—all the streets with little canals of mountain water running along the sides—plenty of people, "business," modernness—yet not without a certain racy wild smack, all its own. A place of fast horses, (many mares with their colts,) and I saw lots of big greyhounds for antelope hunting. Now and then groups of miners, some just come in, some starting out, very picturesque.

One of the papers here interview'd me, and reported me as saying off-hand: "I have lived in or visited all the great cities on the Atlantic third of the republic—Boston, Brooklyn with its hills, New Orleans, Baltimore, stately Washington, broad Philadelphia, teeming Cincinnati and Chicago, and for thirty years in that wonder, wash'd by hurried and glittering tides, my own New York, not only the New World's but the world's city—but, newcomer to Denver as I am, and threading its streets, breathing its air, warm'd by its sunshine, and having what there is of its human as well as aerial ozone flash'd upon me now for only three or four days, I am very much like a man feels sometimes toward certain people he meets with, and warms to, and hardly knows why. I, too, can hardly tell why, but as I enter'd the city in the slight haze of a late September afternoon, and have breath'd its air, and slept well o' nights, and have roam'd or rode leisurely, and watch'd the comers and goers at the hotels, and absorb'd the climatic magnetism of this curiously attractive region, there has steadily grown upon me a feeling of affection for the spot, which, sudden as it is, has become so definite and strong that I must put it on record."

So much for my feeling toward the Queen city of the plains and peaks, where she sits in her delicious rare atmosphere, over 5000 feet above sea-level, irrigated by mountain streams, one way looking east over the prairies for a thousand miles, and having the other, westward, in constant view by day, draped in their violet haze, mountain tops innumerable. Yes, I fell in love with Denver, and even felt a wish to spend my declining and dying days there.

I TURN SOUTH—AND THEN EAST AGAIN.

Leave Denver at 8 A.M. by the Rio Grande RR. going south. Mountains constantly in sight in the apparently near distance, veil'd slightly, but still clear and very grand—their cones, colors, sides, distinct against the sky—hundreds, it seem'd thousands, interminable necklaces of them, their tops and slopes hazed more or less slightly in that blue-gray, under the autumn sun, for over a hundred miles—the most spiritual show of objective Nature I ever beheld, or ever thought possible. Occasionally the light strengthens, making a contrast of yellow-tinged silver on one side, with dark and shaded gray on the other. I took a long look at Pike's peak, and was a little disappointed. (I suppose I had expected something stunning.) Our view over plains to the left stretches amply, with corrals here and there, the frequent cactus and wild sage, and herds of cattle feeding. Thus about 120 miles to Pueblo. At that town we board the comfortable and well-equipt Atchison, Topeka and Santa Fe RR., now striking east.

UNFULFILL'D WANTS—THE ARKANSAS RIVER.

I had wanted to go to the Yellowstone river region—wanted specially to see the National Park, and the geysers and the "hoodoo" or goblin land of that country; indeed, hesitated a little at Pueblo, the turning point—wanted to thread the Veta pass—wanted to go over the Santa Fe trail away southwestward to New Mexico—but turn'd and set my face eastward—leaving behind me whetting glimpse-tastes of southeastern Colorado, Pueblo, Bald mountain, the Spanish peaks, Sangre de

The Spanish Peaks.

Christos, Mile-Shoe-curve (which my veteran friend on the locomotive told me was "the boss railroad curve of the universe,") fort Garland on the plains, Veta, and the three great peaks of the Sierra Blancas.

The Arkansas river plays quite a part in the whole of this region— I see it, or its high-cut rocky northern shore, for miles, and cross and recross it frequently, as it winds and squirms like a snake. The plains vary here even more than usual—sometimes a long sterile stretch of scores of miles—then green, fertile and grassy, an equal length. Some very large herds of sheep. (One wants new words in writing about these plains, and all the inland American West—the terms, *far, large, vast,* &c., are insufficient.)

THE PRAIRIES AND GREAT PLAINS IN POETRY.
(After travelling Illinois, Missouri, Kansas and Colorado.)

Grand as the thought that doubtless the child is already born who will see a hundred millions of people, the most prosperous and advanc'd

of the world, inhabiting these Prairies, the great Plains, and the valley
of the Mississippi, I could not help thinking it would be grander still
to see all those inimitable American areas fused in the alembic of a perfect poem, or other esthetic work, entirely western, fresh and limitless—altogether our own, without a trace or taste of Europe's soil, remi-
niscence, technical letter or spirit. My days and nights, as I travel here—
what an exhilaration!—not the air alone, and the sense of vastness, but
every local sight and feature. Everywhere something characteristic—
the cactuses, pinks, buffalo grass, wild sage—the receding perspective,
and the far circle-line of the horizon all times of day, especially fore-
noon—the clear, pure, cool, rarefied nutriment for the lungs, previously
quite unknown—the black patches and streaks left by surface-conflagra-
tions—the deep-plough'd furrow of the "fire-guard"—the slanting snow-
racks built all along to shield the railroad from winter drifts—the prairie-
dogs and the herds of antelope—the curious "dry rivers"—occasionally
a "dug-out" or corral—Fort Riley and Fort Wallace—those towns of the
northern plains, (like ships on the sea,) Eagle-Tail, Coyotè, Cheyenne,
Agate, Monotony, Kit Carson—with ever the ant-hill and the buffalo-
wallow—ever the herds of cattle and the cow-boys ("cow-punchers") to
me a strangely interesting class, bright-eyed as hawks, with their swarthy
complexions and their broad-brimm'd hats—apparently always on horseback, with loose arms slightly raised and swinging as they ride.

THE SPANISH PEAKS—EVENING ON THE PLAINS.

Between Pueblo and Bent's fort, southward, in a clear afternoon
sun-spell I catch exceptionally good glimpses of the Spanish peaks. We
are in southeastern Colorado—pass immense herds of cattle as our first-
class locomotive rushes us along—two or three times crossing the
Arkansas, which we follow many miles, and of which river I get fine
views, sometimes for quite a distance, its stony, upright, not very high,
palisade banks, and then its muddy flats. We pass Fort Lyon—lots of
adobie houses—limitless pasturage, appropriately fleck'd with those herds
of cattle—in due time the declining sun in the west—a sky of limpid
pearl over all—and so evening on the great plains. A calm, pensive,
boundless landscape—the perpendicular rocks of the north Arkansas,
hued in twilight—a thin line of violet on the southwestern horizon—
the palpable coolness and slight aroma—a belated cow-boy with some

unruly member of his herd—an emigrant wagon toiling yet a little further, the horses slow and tired—two men, apparently father and son, jogging along on foot—and around all the indescribable *chiaroscuro* and sentiment, (profounder than anything at sea,) athwart these endless wilds.

AMERICA'S CHARACTERISTIC LANDSCAPE.

Speaking generally as to the capacity and sure future destiny of that plain and prairie area (larger than any European kingdom) it is the inexhaustible land of wheat, maize, wool, flax, coal, iron, beef and pork, butter and cheese, apples and grapes—land of ten million virgin farms—to the eye at present wild and unproductive—yet experts say that upon it when irrigated may easily be grown enough wheat to feed the world. Then as to scenery (giving my own thought and feeling,) while I know the standard claim is that Yosemite, Niagara falls, the upper Yellowstone and the like, afford the greatest natural shows, I am not so sure but the Prairies and Plains, while less stunning at first sight, last longer, fill the esthetic sense fuller, precede all the rest, and make North America's characteristic landscape.

Indeed through the whole of this journey, with all its shows and varieties, what most impress'd me, and will longest remain with me, are these same prairies. Day after day, and night after night, to my eyes, to all my senses—the esthetic one most of all—they silently and broadly unfolded. Even their simplest statistics are sublime.

EMILY FAITHFULL.

Garden of the Gods.

1884

The name of Emily Faithfull is seldom invoked nowadays in discussions of prominent women of Victorian England, but for a time the clergyman's daughter was an inspiration to all those of her sex who sought to break into occupations long dominated by men. As Elise Boulding recounts in her massive study, *The Underside of History*, "... Faithfull is legendary in English women's history for her success in holding open certain occupational fields for women. [She] opened and ran a successful printing press in the teeth of male insistence that this work was too heavy for women."[5] On three occasions Faithfull's reputation carried her overseas to America to deliver a series of lectures entitled "Woman's Work"—lectures that encouraged women to hold their own in a man's world.

It is thus not surprising that when Emily Faithfull visited Colorado, she sought out the kind of women who reinforced her convictions. Her experiences in the state formed a sizable chapter of her book *Three Visits to America*, and stand as a rare glance at late-nineteenth-century Colorado society from a woman's point of view.

Of course, Faithfull's obsession with the progress of women did not prevent her from succumbing to the beauty and serenity of the Colorado landscape. The normally peripatetic Englishwoman seems to have found in the mountain air and clear skies the kind of nirvana that has drawn the restless westward for nearly 150 years. Indeed, when Faithfull described a "sense of *living*" as an "absolute delight which cannot be realized by those who have never experienced the buoyancy of this electric air," she might have been speaking to soulmates in a later generation who know what it is to be "laid back."

GLIMPSES
OF GLORY

I WATCHED "THE OLD
year out and new year in" under the shadow of the majestic range of
the Rocky Mountains, in the midst of scenery more wild and magnificent
than anything I ever imagined before, more than 6,000 feet above the
level of the sea; yet, thanks to the lightness and purity of the atmosphere, I could breathe there with a freedom seldom vouchsafed to an
asthmatic; and though the thermometer was at zero, such was the power
of the sun during the morning hours, that it was far pleasanter to walk
abroad without a sealskin than with one.

No wonder that invalids have sought Colorado as a land in which
"life *is* worth living," and become enthusiasts about a climate which
is cool in summer and balmy in winter—a place noted for its exquisite
blue skies and transparent atmosphere as well as its grand scenery. Of
course I do not mean to say that there is no bad weather in Colorado,
but it is certainly safe to assert that the belt of country skirting the
eastern base of the Rocky Mountains enjoys an amount of sunshine
and bright weather not to be found in any other section of the United
States; and the mineral springs—hot and cold, sulphur, soda, and iron—
are too numerous to mention, those of Manitou (six miles from this),
Idaho, and Canyon Creek, being most resorted to as specifics for diseases of many kinds.

I left Chicago on Saturday morning, and travelled for two nights
and a day without leaving the cars, chiefly over barren prairies extending for hundreds of miles, across the Missouri by a picturesque bridge,
which I saw to advantage from the opposite bank. Here the track became
more interesting; and at last, shortly before we reached Denver, the
Rocky Mountains came in sight, and for the first time I fully appreciated the illusion of distance. When our train seemed quite close to

the base of these mountains, I learned that we were more than forty miles away!

Denver was chiefly generous to me in the matter of rain. Taking advantage, however, of the first fine day, I drove with Mrs. Olive Wright round the city and on to the hills beyond. Women have always been remarkable for their success with the young of their own species; but in Mrs. Wright I met a lady familiar with all the details of cattle-raising and colt-breaking. We have one lady in London who has turned her attention from the study of the law to the training and selling of horses, and who is well known to the *habituées* of Rotten Row, where she may be seen riding the horses she wishes to sell. There, in the wild life at the foot of the Rocky Mountains, it was not perhaps surprising to meet with a practical advocate of "cattle-raising and colt-breaking as a desirable feminine employment." Nor is Mrs. Wright the first in the field in Colorado. In 1869 a girl of twenty-one alighted from the Denver coach, and secured an office, in which she opened an agency for Singer's sewing-machines. She had been left, at the death of her parents, a mere child in Illinois, without support, and had struck out a line for herself in Chicago. With nothing but her own industry and courage to help her, she secured a position as teacher in the Singer office in that city. When she asked to start a Denver agency, great was the astonishment of her employers; but she had displayed so much business tact they resolved to let her make the attempt. She had energetic men in rival establishments to contend with, but she rose superior to all obstacles, and won a pronounced success. She then married a cattle-dealer whose herds were numbered by thousands; and when he died, leaving her with two young sons, she at once assumed all the vast responsibilities, and became one of the leading cattle-dealers not only of Colorado, but of the United States. Fortune followed every venture she made, and "her income rolled in at the rate of from 100,000 to 300,000 dollars a year." The month before I visited Denver she became the wife of Bishop Warren, but remains proud of the fact that, although she was once so poor, she owes this vast fortune chiefly to her own industry and perseverance.

I was somewhat disappointed, I must confess, in the Windsor Hotel. I suppose when one remembers how the city stands in the midst of an alkali desert—that twenty years ago it was a sparsely-settled village with only log-cabins, in which dwelt people in constant dread of Indians, who were expected to scalp every one in the place before nightfall—it is marvellous to think what has been already accomplished there in such a short space of time, and in the face of such difficulties. The streets are full of activity; there are fine houses and fast horses; carriages are to be seen with heraldic crests familiar to Europeans, but somewhat out of place in this land of equality. "Yes," said a friend, in answer to a remark I made, "it reminds me of the old saying, people nowadays use coats of arms who wore coats without arms a few years back." Considerable extravagance is also to be seen—gorgeous clothes and pretentious entertainments; but at the same time there is energy and liberality— schools have been built, an excellent university opened, and if Denver has the faults, she has also the virtues, of a new wealthy Western city.

The Tabor Opera House justly ranks as one of the finest theatres in America, and I saw it under the best possible circumstances. The Italian Opera Company arrived in Denver during one of my visits there, and Colonel Mapleson kindly invited me to be present on the opening night; so I not only heard Gerster sing, but saw the rank, fashion, and beauty of the city assembled to welcome her. Patti received an immense ovation next day, but I had to leave for Greeley—a town founded by Horace Greeley and his friend Mr. Meeker, on strictly temperance principles. The Indians not only resented the intrusion of the white men, but were rendered furious by the introduction of the agricultural machines they brought with them, and Mr. Meeker soon fell a prey to their vengeance. The *Greeley Tribune* is still conducted by a son of the murdered man. Ralph Meeker is one of the ablest journalists in America. He has travelled so much in Europe and lived so long abroad, knows England, France, and Russia as well as most Londoners know their own city, that he is thoroughly cosmopolitan; and many of his friends would certainly be surprised if they could have a glimpse of his present surroundings, and see him contentedly settling down in a place where the most stirring event is the addition of a new irrigating ditch or the arrival of an itinerant lecturer.

Unfortunately I just missed the meetings of the State Agricultural College at Denver, at which Mrs. Olive Wright read a very interesting paper on "What women are doing in Colorado." Some women seem to be mining; the first prize at the last State fair was taken by a lady for skilful horsemanship and horse-breaking; and much of the value of the domestic cattle industry is, according to her paper, due to them. I certainly heard of girls on the prairies, who seemed to like a tramp over the plains in search of the boundary line of her father's "claim" as much as the daughter of a British sportsman enjoys a morning on a Scotch moor during the grouse-shooting season. They become as used to handling the rifle as the plough, and many of the pioneer ladies I heard of were pursuing their studies in their prairie homes. Some have gone through trials which even would shake the nerves of the sterner sex. I was told of a widow who had built her own "claim shack," had it twice blown away by tornadoes and once burned to the ground in the course of two years; but she holds on to the life she has chosen, and in face and form is the embodiment of health.

From Denver to Colorado Springs the Rocky Mountains seemed to increase in beauty both as to variety of form and color. I shall never forget that morning's journey, with the snow slightly spread on the ground, and sparkling with a thousand colors in the rays of a burning sun, which made the heat of the Pullman car so oppressive that we sought the freedom of the "platform" outside as we crept along on the Denver and Rio Grande Railway through this bewildering maze of ravine-scarred mountains. When I reached my destination I found General Palmer's carriage waiting for me, but, greatly to my disappointment, he and Mrs. Palmer had been suddenly summoned to New York; but their friends, Mr. Elwell and Mrs. Abby Sage Richardson, were ready to welcome me in their place to their beautiful mountain home, Glen Eyrie, about six miles from Colorado Springs. After a wild drive across the "Mesa"—the Spanish for plain—past the Garden of the Gods, I found myself descending an almost perpendicular road, which forcibly suggested a devotional exercise, as well as the prudent course of holding on to the wagonette, and there at the foot I saw a literal realization of Cowper's desire for "a lodge in some vast wilderness," at the entrance of a deep ravine at the foot of Pike's Peak—a region already well known to English readers through Bret Harte, and Colonel John Hay's "Pike County Ballads." The lodge gates opened at our approach, and after a drive of considerable length up this wild canyon, amid fantastic vermilion-colored rocks a hundred feet high, we came to the stables, and then another turn in the road gave me a full view of the picturesque house General Palmer built in this romantic gorge some ten years ago, much to the dissatisfaction of the Indians, who watched the process with considerable indignation at the white man's encroachment on their territory, but wisely abandoned their wigwams, and retired from the fruitless struggle into Mexico and elsewhere.

It seems very strange to find in the midst of this wild country, and in the very heart of this ravine, so perfectly appointed a house, and to spend our Christmas Day after the Old World fashion—a splendid Christmas tree having been decked out with the usual bonbons, presents,

The Great Hall at Glen Eyrie Castle.

and gay-colored candles, and placed in the library for the special benefit of the eldest little daughter of the house, who had not only many gifts herself, but had prepared presents for all the servants and children of the retainers on the estate, who trooped in freely at the appointed hour, taking their places on the sofas and arm-chairs with the true American spirit of brotherhood and equality, which even the English butler and other servants from across the Atlantic seemed to share. Then came a dinner for the "grown-up" guests, with the usual crackers, apt quotations from Gilbert's famous "Bab Ballad" about the origin of the strange mottoes found therein, and after a due amount of startling tales of adventure by land and sea, and witty local stories, the piano came into request, and a German lady staying in the house "discoursed sweet music," and some Christmas carols sung by her daughters concluded our evening's entertainment. Seldom have I heard Beethoven, Chopin, and Mendelsohn better interpreted by even professional players.

I must record one very remarkable incident of that Christmas Day.

A great storm of wind swept over the Colorado plains, and even managed to effect an entrance into this weird but secluded nook. It shook the house to its very foundation, and it was fortunate that all the guests had arranged to stay till the next day, for no one could have crossed the Mesa on so wild a night. We really trembled for the chimneys, the hothouses and the conservatories, but, strange to relate, no damage was done. As morning dawned the wind ceased, and the dazzling sun tempted all lovers of outdoor exercise into the pathless woods and up the mountain-sides; but when the news of the outer world reached us, no one was surprised to hear that a few miles away a freight train of nine heavily-loaded cars had been blown off the railway track at Monument Park, a place which is exposed to the full force of the wind as it sweeps in its mad career over plains extending hundreds of miles.

I used the expression, *news from the outer world,* advisedly, for no postman desecrated the mountain seclusion of Glen Eyrie. If the mail-bag was wanted, a mountain messenger had to be sent to Colorado Springs, and no New York paper reached there till it was five days old. My dependence upon the morning newspaper has been a standing joke against me; for ever since I learned to take an interest in matters beyond the home which first sheltered me, I have always regarded it as quite as essential to my well-being as my breakfast, and never before had I found myself totally unable to procure this adjunct to a comfortable existence. Not even the little sheet published in Colorado Springs could reach Glen Eyrie by the accustomed breakfast-hour. Strange to say, in that new land, amid those new sights and associations, I found myself settling down to this novel state of things with the utmost composure, though, I confess, the opening of the mail-bag, with the possibilities of English newspapers and letters, was always an event creating great excitement, and a New Year's greeting from dear old Manchester, in the shape of some photographs, was a welcome and opportune arrival on the very day itself, when the messenger returned early in the afternoon, after making a special expedition to the post-office on my behalf.

As the days passed by in far too swift succession, the better I appreciated the enthusiasm of those who had made Colorado, with its marvelous mountains, prairies, lakes, and waterfalls, their home, and no one could be admitted into the delightful society to be found in the unique town of Colorado Springs without being impressed with the fact that it is a most cosmopolitan, as well as cultured community, drawn from all parts of the earth. The "far West," so often represented as a "wilderness," given over to the reign of the wild "riotous ranchman," where a race of ignorant backwoodsmen can alone be expected, is in reality peopled by the adventurous sons of Britain, and young collegians from the more crowded Eastern States of America. Colorado Springs is, in fact, a very exceptional place, for its wonderful health-giving properties have attracted some of the best people from other cities, and it is really a charming resort. The streets are lined with trees—there are more than 7,000 in this small town—and there are few days in the year when even invalids can not venture out of doors. The dryness of the ground, the electric air, and the bright warm sunshine render croquet and tennis pleasurable pursuits even in winter. No liquor can be sold, as every deed of land contains the forfeiture clause; nevertheless wine is to be found on the tables of the hospitable and wealthy inhabitants.

One of the best doctors in Colorado Springs is an Englishman, a nephew of Mr. Solly, who has done so much for working-men's clubs in England. Dr. Solly is quite the leading spirit of this Western colony, first and foremost in every progressive measure. "Renting out rooms" used to be a feature of life at the Springs, but latterly it has proved quite insufficient to accommodate the invalids and tourists who come in increasing numbers every year. "In fact," said Dr. Solly, "the problem I have had to solve has been *how to house the outcast rich*," and the building of the Antlers Hotel was the way in which that difficulty was met. Scotch enterprise came to the assistance of the project in the person of Mr. James Caird, of Dundee, and a handsome house of quarry-faced lava stone, capable of holding more than 100 persons, with broad piazzas commanding a lovely view of the surrounding mountains, was opened about two years ago. It is managed by a lady, who has shown singular executive ability, and I shall always remember with pleasure the days I spent in "the bridal suite," which was very handsomely assigned for my use during my stay there.

The windows of my sitting-room looked out on the mountains, the lofty summit of Pike's Peak, 14,300 feet high, towering above them all. As I write now in the noise and smoke of London, I vividly recall the hours spent in watching the marvellous panoramic changes that passed over the scene before me then. The rosy tints at dawn, the intense blue, the exquisite golden glow of sunset, and the great peaks standing out like weird, majestic phantoms through those clear, starlight nights.

The day after I had taken up my abode at the Antlers, Miss Warren, the manager, called to see if I had everything I required in the hotel. During the conversation which ensued she surprised me by saying that she had reason "to be very grateful" to me. "How could this be, considering I had never seen her before in my life?" was my natural rejoinder. Then followed the strange and pleasing explanation. She had been at Cincinnati during the great flood of 1883, and was in some doubt as to the wisdom of undertaking the responsible position offered her at the Antlers. She was feeling too dispirited to believe in her capacity for properly filling the novel post of manager. She could not even purchase the hotel furniture she had gone there to buy, for the town was almost in darkness, and the inhabitants were full of the calamity that had come upon them. During that period she saw my lecture on "Woman's Work" advertised, and she resolved to hear it. It appears that I made some remarks that inspired her with courage, and enabled her to see her way clear before her. She determined to enter upon the work she subsequently carried on with so much credit to herself and satisfaction to her employers, and often had she wished to thank me for the encouragement so unwittingly given on that occasion. Earnest workers, engaged in public work of any description, will appreciate the feelings with which I received such unexpected testimony, for they know how very futile, and easily dispensed with, seem one's best efforts, and will readily understand how such a definite proof of help afforded to some unknown conscientious but doubting heart not only renews your own hope, but stimulates you to fresh activity.

Twelve years ago there was hardly a house to be seen in Colorado Springs, and it owes its existence entirely to General Palmer's enterprise. The town site was bought for 1 dollar and 25 cents an acre; today residence lots of 50 feet cost about 2,000 dollars and business lots of 25 feet are worth 5,000 dollars. Why it should have been called Colorado *Springs* I can not tell, for it possesses none; these, however, are to be found five miles off, at Manitou (which preserves its Indian name, "Spirit of the Waters"), where the celebrated soda and iron springs abound, and a flourishing town has also sprung up. Canon Kingsley spent much of his time in America as the guest of Dr. Bell, a London physician, who settled at Manitou, after aiding General Palmer in his long explorations through this region, long before the Indians and buffaloes had departed and the trains had arrived.

In 1870, when General Palmer projected the Denver and Rio Grande Railway, the largest city in the huge State of Colorado could scarcely claim 5,000 inhabitants, and the entire population of the vast State was only 40,000; yet hardly were 1,200 miles of railway built, when new cities throughout Colorado developed with surprising rapidity. In this remote mountain region of the "Springs," the capital of El Paso county, is now found a town capable of supporting an endowed college, eight churches, a handsome club, and an opera-house, at which there is a fair stock company. Good travelling theatrical combinations often visit it. I found the Boston Ideal Opera Company in possession last New Year's Day, and it is always crammed from floor to ceiling for amateur entertainments, which are as popular in this isolated Western sanitorium as in the more robust cities in the Eastern States. Theatrical enterprises for the benefit of local charities usually take place under the generalship of Dr. Solly, who is not only a very clever actor, but a first-rate manager. This active, public-spirited gentleman spares no pains to have dresses and cast as perfect as he can make them. Rehearsals are carried on day after day as carefully as if the amateur players depended for their daily bread upon the success of the play they have undertaken to produce. An ambitious but really admirable performance of "The Wolf in Sheep's Clothing" came off during my stay there, in which Miss Stretell—sister-in-law of Comyns Carr of "Far from the Madding Crowd" and "Called Back" dramatic notoriety—greatly distinguished herself. Considering how large a proportion of the inhabitants of Colorado Springs are regarded as invalids, I was absolutely astonished at the gaiety which prevailed in this secluded nook among the mountains. There were not only literary debating clubs, popular lectures, select poetical readings by Mrs. Abby Sage Richardson (one of the best read, most cultured ladies I ever met), but dinners, picnics, and, last but not least, balls, which were kept up with great spirit long after the sun arose the next morning!

The marked features of the Colorado climate are the dry air and clear sunlight. President Tenney told me that, according to the observation of six consecutive years, there was an average of 300 clear and fine days in each. No wonder that the breathless asthmatic or consumptive patient exclaims, with Shakespeare's heroine in the Forest of Arden, "I like this place, and willingly would spend my time in it." I believe that P. T. Barnum once said that the Colorado people were the most disappointed he ever saw. "Two-thirds of them came here to die," he exclaimed, *and they can't do it!* This wonderful air brings them back from the verge of the tomb." But the region of the Rocky Mountains offers inducements of many other kinds: the active man finds boundless opportunities in cattle ranches, sheep-keeping, and horse-raising, to say nothing of the coal, iron, lead, silver, and even gold with which

Manitou and Pikes Peak.

the State abounds; while the sportsman is attracted by the wild deer, antelope, and elk, and more dangerous game in the shape of wolves and bears, which still infest the forests of pine and cedar. How the heart of "Red Spinner" would rejoice in the trout-fishing to be found in the neighborhood of Lord Dunraven's estate, "Estes Park," and revel in the speckled beauties of the finny tribe that haunt the streams and lakes of Colorado! While the invalid is restored to health by the mineral springs and the soft yet exhilarating air, the overworked merchant from some crowded city also finds the completest freedom from letters, tele-grams, and newspapers in the recesses of these mountains, where there is indeed "a solitude where none intrude." The signal station on Pike's Peak is said to be the highest habitation in the world. Little we think as we read "the weather probabilities" of how the men on that snow-bound rocky summit, 2,000 miles west of New York, flash down the mountain-side and over the wild prairies of America, the information gathered from the signs they have learned to interpret by the use of the meteorological instruments which have found their way to that wild outpost.

It is impossible to convey any idea of "The Garden of the Gods," with its massive red sandstone portals, 380 feet high, the various wild mountain passes, Rainbow Falls, or the Cheyenne Canyon (the Spanish for ravine); and who in England would believe in *a frozen waterfall?* Yet that was one of the strange sights witnessed during an expedition over the Ute Pass.

It will be equally difficult, I expect, for friends at home to imagine a picnic in winter, with snow-capped mountains around, frozen streams across which carriages could even venture in safety, and yet a sun so hot that overcoats and sealskins were dispensed with as a merry party discussed an excellent luncheon under the shade of the pine-trees, in which blue jay birds were perched. Such was the *al fresco* repast I enjoyed on the 12th of January, thanks to the hospitality of President Tenney. And this was but an episode in a delightful day's excursion far away in the depths of the Cheyenne Canyon, among wondrous rocks of black, gray, and bright red sandstone, often vivid with patches of yellow and green lichen. Sometimes we were looking at waterfalls, or peering into vast fantastic chasms, and at other moments gazing at the perpendicular rocks towering above our heads. Every moment was "a picture for re-membrance."

I must candidly confess that during my tour through Colorado "a change came o'er the spirit of my dream," and Nature obtained a hold over me in those Rocky Mountains she had never had before. My early years were spent in the country, but I soon learned to love the town. I became a thorough Londoner at heart. Humanity had an attraction for me that nature never possessed; men and women, with their struggles, hopes, and fears, interested me far more than the finest landscape; with them I ever felt a sympathy and companionship that land and sea could not inspire—in fact, the lonely mountain and the restless wave beating without result on the unresponsive shore used often to fill me with a depression I could not endure. But Colorado scenery, combined with such a glorious climate, at last "enthused" me, as our Yankee cousins would call it. The very sense of *living* was an absolute delight which can not be realized by those who have never experienced the buoyancy of this electric air. I had often before wondered how cultured young men, with the results of hundreds of years of civilization within their reach, could relinquish them for the privations of primeval life in the wilds of Australia and America. Now I understood something of the compensation of "God's free air," even on a cattle ranche far away from the enjoyments of art and literature; and the feeling deepened during my trip over the Rocky Mountains, through the marvellous Grand Canyon of the Arkansas, after I left Colorado Springs.

I started by an early morning train to Pueblo, and branched off on the Leadville line which brought me to what the inhabitants of this great Republic have well named the Royal Gorge. Mr. Ruskin's heart would indeed have ached to see the solemnity and majesty of this weird ravine desecrated by the noisy, ugly, puffing locomotive which drew our train through its mystic shades by the side of the river, under the giant cliffs 3,000 feet high, that seemed to frown on its intrusive presence, and even to threaten its puny form with destruction!

The giant of the nineteenth century—the ogre who, while he brings these lovely places within ordinary reach, spoils their picturesqueness and destroys their solitude—is gradually asserting his sway throughout this wild district. Slowly but surely he is even winding his stealthy way, 14,220 feet above the sea-level, up Pike's Peak itself. How Colorado will hereafter be affected by this railroad I really can not say; but it is certain there are few Americans left who love the wild forests and mountains well enough to protest, like their countryman Thoreau, against railways, steamboats, and telegraphs. The trail of this restless, nervous, bustling, mammon-worshipping age is over all; the spirit which ani-

mates Wall Street asserts itself in the wild canyons of the Rocky Mountains, and many a dollar-loving inhabitant of Manitou is now rejoicing
at the prospective "increase of tourists." People who have hitherto
refrained from making this grand ascent on mules, as involving too much
time and exertion, are expected to avail themselves of the iron horse,
which in a few months will be disturbing the serenity of the eagles,
hawks, and coyotes, who have until now shared with the signal station
the possession of the grandest peak of the American Alps.

I reached Salida at six o'clock one evening, and have great reason
to rejoice that my bones are not reposing there at this minute. In the
ordinary reckless American fashion, our train came to a standstill on
the centre lines, facing the depôt, instead of drawing up to a respectable platform on which passengers could alight with ease and safety.
The smallest country railway station in Great Britain is furnished with
this necessary appendage of safe travel, but across the ocean, platforms
are luxuries rarely indulged in! Accordingly I had to step out of the
Pullman car in the middle of the track, and naturally at once proceeded
to cross the lines to the depôt, never noticing in the deepening shades
of evening that another train was coming up. But for the timely inter-
vention of a stranger, who kindly but very uncomfortably seized me
by the throat, I most certainly should have been run over by the locomotive, if not killed on the spot, for the engine steamed past as he held
me firmly, in his saving but surprising grasp. Nothing strikes the English traveller with more dismay than the heedless disregard of life in
America. The railway tracks are unprotected; they often run through
the busiest streets, killing foot-passengers and scaring horses with equal
impartiality. On the prairies, dead cows and horses on the track are
of course facts of daily occurrence; indeed all the locomotives are provided with "cow-catchers." Certainly, in places "where men most do
congregate" a placard greets the eye, "When the bell rings, look out for
the locomotive"; but as the train dashes past your carriage as you wait
at some dry-goods store, "Deaths on the Track" is naturally a standing
heading for a daily paragraph in American newspapers.

Salida is a sheltered village into which no snow ever penetrates, and
the air was so soft and balmy that I stayed on the balcony of the hotel
that January evening watching in the moonlight the famous Sangre de
Criste range of mountains. After resting till four o'clock, I started without any breakfast, or the comforts of a Pullman car, in order to see
the sun rise over the celebrated Marshall Pass. Never shall I forget that
journey. No pen or pencil can ever do justice to the scenes through

which we passed. The Denver and Rio Grande Railway is indeed a very marvel of engineering skill. The man who planned it seems to have lassoed the mountains and caught them in a tangle of coils. The single track winds round and round in curves so sharp that from our middle compartment we could see the engine in front of us, as well as the rear carriage, and far ahead was our pilot-engine, looking like a child's toy in the midst of this grand landscape, which was only married by the inevitable snowsheds, the one near the summit being just four miles long. No human being inhabits this wild region save coyotes, bears, and eagles, and the men who live in huts along the track, to see that it is cleared of the falling boulders from the rocks above. At last we reached an elevation of 10,857 feet, the highest railway track in America, and witnessed a glorious sunrise. Then began our descent on the other side, five hours bringing us to Gunnison. After this we entered the Black Canyon, where the rocks are as high as those of the Royal Gorge, and the chasm wider. Another climb by a steep grade—213 feet to the mile—and we were at Cedar Divide; before me lay the Uncompahgre Valley and the Wahsatch Mountains beyond. At the Grande Junction a veritable desert of 150 miles of prairie had to be traversed; our train struck on a mining camp at which there had been an accident, and stopped to take four injured men "on board," to procure them medical help at the nearest town.

The sunset that evening was a worthy pendant to the sunrise seen at the Marshall Pass: the last glorious rays of the departing sun lighted up the peaks and snowy summits of the mountains with a brilliancy of color no artist would dare, even were it possible, to represent on canvas; and then, as there is no twilight here, darkness quickly ensued, the Pullman car was lighted up, the porter began to make the beds, and before ten o'clock every one was comfortably sleeping, while the train sped on through the night, and landed us at six o'clock the following morning at Salt Lake City. If travellers from New York to San Francisco care to enjoy some of the grandest scenery in the world, they will abandon the old road across the dull prairies. Branch off at Denver by this new route, and there is an everchanging panorama of snow-crowned mountains, deep gorges, forest-covered slopes, and a remembrance for a lifetime. Even those to whom the Alps, the Andes, and the Himalayas are familiar, will appreciate the glimpses of glory to be obtained as they stand on the brink of those terrible precipices during a railroad journey over the Rocky Mountains.

RUDYARD KIPLING.

1889

Of Rudyard Kipling's initial visit to America in 1889, his eminent biographer, Lord Birkenhead, has written: "In spite of his intellectual development, Kipling was callow and insolent. He gave brash interviews to journalists, and lost his temper with American porters at the Customs House [in San Francisco], who responded to his demand for service with far less alacrity than his Indian bearers."[6]

The precocious young writer may be forgiven his insolence. At the time of his visit to the U.S., the twenty-four year-old Englishman was already an established journalist in India and author of two books. Moreover, the account of his trip across America, *From Sea to Sea*, probably stands as the single most brilliant piece of invective ever unloaded on late-nineteenth-century American life. Kipling's descriptions of Americans and their land are precious: American language is "wild advertisement, gas, bunkum"; a woman he meets on the train is "muzzy with beer"; hailstones (avoiding contemporary comparisons to marbles, golf balls, and grapefruits) are as "big as the top of a sherry glass." There is no doubt that Kipling truly believed in the supremacy of the British Empire, and that America suffered in the comparison, so the unleashing of his devastating wit on the rawness of the New World was probably an inevitable consequence of his visit. Colorado was not spared.

THE MAN
WITH SORROW

T HE HEAT WAS STIFLING.
We quitted the desert and launched into the rolling green plains of Colorado. Dozing uneasily with every removable rag removed, I was roused
by a blast of intense cold and the drumming of a hundred drums. The
train had stopped. Far as the eye could range the land was white under
two feet of hail—each hailstone as big as the top of a sherry-glass. I saw
a young colt by the side of the track standing with his poor little fluffy
back to the pitiless pelting. He was pounded to death. An old horse
met his doom on the run. He galloped wildly towards the train, but
his hind legs dropped into a hole half water and half ice. He beat the
ground with his fore-feet for a minute, and then rolling over on his
side submitted quietly to be killed.

When the storm ceased, we picked our way cautiously and crippledly
over a track that might give way at any moment. The Western driver
urges his train much as does the Subaltern the bounding pony, and,
'twould seem, with an equal sense of responsibility. If a foot does go
wrong, why there you are, don't you know, and if it is all right, why
all right it is, don't you know. But I would sooner be on the pony than
the train.

This seems a good place wherein to preach on American versatility.
When Mr. Howells writes a novel, when a reckless hero dams a flood
by heaving a dynamite-shattered mountain into it, or when a notoriety-
hunting preacher marries a couple in a balloon, you shall hear the great
American press rise on its hind legs and walk round mouthing over
the versatility of the American citizen. And he is versatile—horribly
so. The unlimited exercise of the right of private judgment (which, by
the way, is a weapon not one man in ten is competent to handle), his
blatant cocksureness, and the dry-air-bred restlessness that makes him

crawl all over the furniture when he is talking to you, conspire to make him versatile. But what he calls versatility the impartial bystander of Anglo-Indian extraction is apt to deem mere casualness, and dangerous casualness at that. No man can grasp the inwardness of an employ by the light of pure reason—even though that reason be republican. He must serve an apprenticeship to one craft and learn that craft all the days of his life if he wishes to excel therein. Otherwise he merely "puts the thing through somehow"; and occasionally he doesn't. But wherein lies the beauty of this form of mental suppleness? Old man California, whom I shall love and respect always, told me one or two anecdotes about American versatility and its consequences that came back to my mind with direful force as the train progressed. We didn't upset, but I don't think that that was the fault of the driver or the men who made the track. Take up—you can easily find them—the accounts of ten consecutive railway catastrophes—not little accidents, but first-class fatalities, when the long cars turn over, take fire, and roast the luckless occupants alive. To seven out of the ten you shall find appended the cheerful statement: "The accident is supposed to have been due to the rails spreading." That means the metals were spiked down to the ties with such versatility that the spikes or the tracks drew under the constant vibration of the traffic and the metals opened out. No one is hanged for these little affairs.

We began to climb hills, and then we stopped—at night in darkness, while men threw sand under the wheels and crowbarred the track and then "guessed" that we might proceed. Not being in the least anxious to face my Maker half asleep and rubbing my eyes, I went forward to a common car, and was rewarded by two hours' conversation with the stranded, broken-down, husband-abandoned actress of a fourth-rate, stranded, broken-down, manager-bereft company. She was muzzy with beer, reduced to her last dollar, fearful that there would be no one to meet her at Omaha, and wept at intervals because she had given the conductor a five-dollar bill to change, and he hadn't come back. He was an Irishman, so I knew he couldn't steal, and I addressed myself to the task of consolation. I was rewarded, after a decent interval, by the history of a life so wild, so mixed, so desperately improbable, and yet so simply probable, and above all so quick—not fast—in its kaleidoscopic changes that the "Pioneer" would reject any summary of it. And so you will never know how she, the beery woman with the tangled blonde hair, was once a girl on a farm in far-off New Jersey. How he, a travelling actor, had wooed and won her—"but Paw he was always set against Alf"—and how he and she embarked all their little capital on the word of a faithless manager who disbanded his company a hundred miles from nowhere, and how she and Alf and a third person who had not yet made any noise in the world, had to walk the railway-track and beg from the farm-houses; how that third person arrived and went away again with a wail, and how Alf took to the whisky and other things still more calculated to make a wife unhappy; and how after barn-stormings, insults, shooting-scrapes, and pitiful collapses of poor companies she had once won an encore. It was not a cheerful tale to listen to. There was a real actress in the Pullman—such an one as travels sumptuously with a maid and dressing-case—and my draggle-tail thought of appealing to her for help, but broke down after several attempts to walk into the car jauntily as befitted a sister in the profession. Then the conductor reappeared—the five-dollar bill honestly changed—and she wept by reason of beer and gratitude together, and then fell asleep waveringly, alone in the car, and became almost beautiful and quite kissable; while the Man with the Sorrow stood at the door between actress and actress and preached grim sermons on the certain end of each if they did not mend their ways and find regeneration through the miracle of the Baptist creed. Yes, we were a queer company going up to the Rockies together. I was the luckiest, because when a breakdown occurred, and we were delayed for twelve hours, I ate all the Baptist's sample biscuits. They were various in composition, but nourishing. Always travel with a drummer.

After much dallying and more climbing we came to a pass like all the Bolan Passes in the world, and the Black Cañon of the Gunnison called they it. We had been climbing for very many hours, and attained a modest elevation of some seven or eight thousand feet above the sea, when we entered a gorge, remote from the sun, where the rocks were two thousand feet sheer, and where a rock-splintered river roared and howled ten feet below a track which seemed to have been built on the simple principle of dropping miscellaneous dirt into the river and pinning a few rails atop. There was a glory and a wonder and a mystery about that mad ride which I felt keenly (you will find it properly dressed up in the guide-books), until I had to offer prayers for the safety of the train. There was no hope of seeing the track two hundred yards ahead. We seemed to be running into the bowels of the earth at the invitation of an irresponsible stream. Then the solid rock would open and disclose a curve of awful twistfulness. Then the driver put on all steam, and we would go round that curve on one wheel chiefly, the Gunnison River gnashing its teeth below. The cars overhung the edge of the water, and if a single one of the rails had chosen to spread, nothing in the wide world could have saved us from drowning. I knew we should damage something in the end—the sombre horrors of the gorge, the rush of the jade-green water below, and the cheerful tales told by the conductor made me certain of the catastrophe.

We had just cleared the Black Cañon and another gorge, and were sailing out into open country nine thousand feet above the level of the sea, when we came most suddenly round a corner upon a causeway across a waste water—half dam and half quarry-pool. The locomotive gave one wild "Hoo! Hoo! Hoo!" but it was too late. He was a beautiful bull, and goodness only knows why he had chosen the track for a constitutional with his wife. *She* was flung to the left, but the cowcatcher caught *him,* and turning him round, hove him shoulder deep into the pool. The expression of blank, blind bewilderment on his bovine, jovine face was wonderful to behold. He was not angry. I don't

"After much dallying and more climbing we came to a pass like all the Bolan passes in the world, and the Black Cañon of the Gunnison called they it."

think he was even scared, though he must have flown ten yards through the air. All he wanted to know was: "Will somebody have the goodness to tell a respectable old gentleman what in the world, or out of it, has occurred?" And five minutes later the stream that had been snapping at our heels in the gorges split itself into a dozen silver threads on a breezy upland, and became an innocent trout-beck, and we halted at a half-dead city, the name of which does not remain with me. It had originally been built on the crest of a wave of prosperity. Once ten thousand people had walked its street; but the boom had collapsed. The great brick houses and the factories were empty. The population lived in little timber shanties on the fringes of the deserted town. There were some railway workshops and things, and the hotel (whose pavement formed the platform of the railway) contained one hundred and more rooms—empty. The place, in its half-inhabitedness, was more desolate than Amber or Chitor. But a man said: "Trout—six pounds—two miles away," and the Sorrowful Man and myself went in search of 'em. The town was ringed by a circle of hills all alive with little thunder-storms that broke across the soft green of the plain in wisps and washes of smoke and amber.

To our tiny party associated himself a lawyer from Chicago. We foregathered on the question of flies, but I didn't expect to meet Elijah Pogram in the flesh. He delivered orations on the future of England and America, and of the Great Federation that the years will bring forth when America and England will belt the globe with their linked hands. According to the notions of the British, he made an ass of himself, but for all his high-falutin he talked sense. I might knock through England on a four months' tour and not find a man capable of putting into words the passionate patriotism that possessed the little Chicago lawyer. And he was a man with points, for he offered me three days' shooting in Illinois, if I would step out of my path a little. I might travel for ten years up and down England ere I found a man who would give a complete stranger so much as a sandwich, and for twenty ere I squeezed as much enthusiasm out of a Britisher. He and I talked politics and trout-flies all one sultry day as we wandered up and down the shallows of the stream aforesaid. Little fish are sweet. I spent two hours whipping a ripple for a fish that I knew was there, and in the pasture-scented dusk caught a three-pounder on a ragged old brown hackle and landed him after ten minutes' excited argument. He was a beauty. If ever any man works the Western trout-streams, he would do well to bring out with him the dingiest flies he possesses. The natives laugh at the tiny English hooks, but they hold, and duns and drabs and sober greys seem to tickle the aesthetic tastes of the trout. For salmon (but don't say that I told you) use the spoon—gold on one side, silver on the other. It is as killing as is a similar article with fish of another calibre. The natives seem to use much too coarse tackle.

It was a search for a small boy who should know the river that revealed to me a new phase of life—slack, slovenly, and shiftless, but very interesting. There was a family in a packing-case hut on the out-skirts of the town. They had seen the city when it was on the boom and made pretence of being the metropolis of the Rockies; and when the boom was over, they had not gone. She was affable, but deeply coated with dirt; he was grim and grimy, and the little children were simply caked with filth of various descriptions. But they lived in a cer-tain sort of squalid luxury, six or eight of them in two rooms; and they enjoyed the local society. It was their eight-year-old son whom I tried to take out with me, but he had been catching trout all his life and "guessed he didn't feel like coming," though I proffered him six shil-lings for what ought to have been a day's pleasuring. "I'll stay with Maw," he said, and from that attitude I could not move him. Maw didn't attempt to argue with him. "If he says he won't come, he won't," she said, as though he were one of the elemental forces of nature instead of a spank-able brat; and "Paw," lounging by the store, refused to interfere. Maw told me that she had been a school-teacher in her not-so-distant youth, but did not tell me what I was dying to know—how she arrived at this mucky tenement at the back of beyond, and why. Though preserving the prettiness of her New England speech, she had come to regard wash-ing as a luxury. Paw chewed tobacco and spat from time to time. Yet, when he opened his mouth for other purposes, he spoke like a well-educated man. There was a story there, but I couldn't get at it.

Next day the Man with the Sorrow and myself and a few others began the real ascent of the Rockies; up to that time our climbing didn't count. The train ran violently up a steep place and was taken to pieces. Five cars were hitched on to two locomotives, and two cars to one loco-motive. This seemed to be a kind and thoughtful act, but I was idiot enough to go forward and watch the coupling-on of the two rear cars in which Caesar and his fortunes were to travel. Some one had lost or eaten the regularly ordained coupling, and a man picked up from the tailboard of the engine a single iron link about as thick as a fetter-link watch-chain, and "guessed it would do." Get hauled up a Simla cliff by the hook of a lady's parasol if you wish to appreciate my sentiments when the cars moved uphill and the link drew tight. Miles away and two thousand feet above our heads rose the shoulder of a hill epauletted with the long line of a snow-tunnel. The first section of the cars crawled a quarter of a mile ahead of us, the track snaked and looped behind, and there was a black drop to the left. So we went up and up and up till the thin air grew thinner and the *chunk-chunk-chunk* of the labouring locomotive was answered by the oppressed beating of the exhausted heart. Through the chequed light and shade of the snow sheds (horrible caverns of rude timbering) we ground our way, halting now and again to allow a down-train to pass. One monster of forty mineral-cars slid past, scarce held by four locomotives, their brakes screaming and chortling in chorus; and in the end, after a glimpse at half America spread mapwise leagues below us, we halted at the head of the longest snow sheds of all, on the crest of the divide, between ten and eleven thousand feet above the level of the sea. The locomotive wished to draw breath, and the passengers to gather the flowers that nodded impertinently through the chinks of the boarding. A lady passenger's nose began to bleed, and other ladies threw themselves down on the seats and gasped with the gasping train, while a wind as keen as a knife-edge rioted down the grimy tunnel.

Then, despatching a pilot-engine to clear the way, we began the downward portion of the journey with every available brake on, and frequent shrieks, till after some hours we reached the level plain, and later the city of Denver, where the Man with the Sorrow went his way and left me to journey on to Omaha alone, after one hasty glance at Denver. The pulse of that town was too like the rushing mighty wind in the Rocky Mountain tunnel. It made me tired because complete strangers desired me to do something to mines which were in mountains, and to purchase building blocks upon inaccessible cliffs; and once, a woman urged that I should supply her with strong drinks. I had almost forgotten that such attacks were possible in any land, for the outward and visible signs of public morality in American towns are generally safe-guarded. For that I respect this people.

Curecanti Needle.

THEODORE ROOSEVELT.

1905

So remarkable was Theodore Roosevelt's diverse life as a politician, president, naturalist, ranchman, warrior, and peacemaker that it is impossible to do him justice in a few brisk paragraphs. But for Coloradans Roosevelt's significance can be narrowed down to a single, salient accomplishment: his order in 1905 creating 14 separate forest reserves throughout the state, part of a plan that resulted in 150 such reserves nationwide. In a posthumous and belated tribute to Roosevelt's unparalleled contributions to conservation, Congress in 1932 changed the name of Colorado National Forest in the northern part of the state to Roosevelt National Forest.

Unlike many other national figures who either by political pressure or conscience created the public lands, Roosevelt's knowledge of the Colorado landscape was first-hand. Twice during his presidency he made extended hunting trips west of the Continental Divide, and both trips were described with Roosevelt's familiar gusto for the popular journals of the day. The article reprinted here recounts Roosevelt's adventures as he hunted bear west of Glenwood Springs with his companion, Dr. Philip Stewart of Colorado Springs.

Those who are not familiar with Roosevelt's outdoor writings will find that his so-called "hunting stories" were more than the usual tale of pursuit and carnage. For this article reveals to the reader what is not widely appreciated about Roosevelt: he was a skilled observer of wildlife who rarely failed to pause and take in the natural world around him. In his tale of the Colorado bear hunt Roosevelt recites a veritable catalog of birds and beasts common to the state, and in the process proves that naturalist John Burroughs was probably right when he claimed that "Amid all his absorbing interests and masterful activities in other fields, his interest and authority in practical natural history are by no means the least."[7]

A COLORADO
BEAR HUNT

IN MID-APRIL, NINETEEN
hundred and five, our party, consisting of Philip B. Stewart, of Colorado Springs, and Dr. Alexander Lambert, of New York, in addition
to myself, left Newcastle, Col., for a bear hunt. As guides and hunters
we had John Goff and Jake Borah, than whom there are no better men
at their work of hunting bear in the mountains with hounds. Each
brought his own dogs; all told, there were twenty-six hounds, and four
half-blood terriers to help worry the bear when at bay. We travelled
in comfort, with a big pack train, spare horses for each of us, and a cook,
packers, and horse wranglers. I carried one of the new model Springfield
military rifles, a 30-40, with a soft-nosed bullet—a very accurate and
hard-hitting gun.

This first day we rode about twenty miles to where camp was
pitched on the upper waters of East Divide Creek. It was a picturesque
spot. At this altitude it was still late winter and the snow lay in drifts,
even in the creek bottom, while the stream itself was not yet clear from
ice. The tents were pitched in a grove of leafless aspens and great spruces,
beside the rushing, ice-rimmed brook. The cook tent, with its stove,
was an attractive place on the cool mornings and in stormy weather.
Fry, the cook, a most competent man, had rigged up a table, and we
had folding camp-chairs—luxuries utterly unknown to my former
camping trips. Each day we breakfasted early and dined ten or twelve
hours later, on returning from the day's hunt; and as we carried no
lunch, the two meals were enjoyed with ravenous pleasure by the entire
company. The horses were stout, tough, shaggy beasts, of wonderful
staying power, and able to climb like cats. The country was very steep
and rugged; the mountain-sides were greasy and slippery from the
melting snow, while the snow bucking through the deep drifts on their

tops and on the north sides was exhausting. Only sure-footed animals could avoid serious tumbles, and only animals of great endurance could have lasted through the work. Both Johnny Goff and his partner, Brick Wells, who often accompanied us on the hunts, were frequently mounted on animals of uncertain temper, with a tendency to buck on insufficient provocation; but they rode them with entire indifference up and down any incline. One of the riders, "Al," a very good tempered man, a tireless worker, had as one of his horses a queer, big-headed dun beast, with a black stripe down its back and traces of zebra-like bands on the backs of his front legs. He was an atavistic animal, looking much as the horses must have looked which an age or two ago lived in this very locality and were preyed on by sabre-toothed tigers, hyenadons, and other strange and terrible beasts of a long-vanished era. Lambert remarked to him: "Al, you ought to call that horse of yours 'Fossil'; he is a hundred thousand years old." To which Al, with immovable face, replied: "Gee! and that man sold him to me for a seven-year-old! I'll have the law on him!"

The hounds were most interesting, and showed all the variations of character and temper to be expected in such a pack; a pack in which performance counted for everything and pedigree for nothing. One of the best hounds was half fox terrier. Three of Johnny's had been with us four years before, when he and I hunted cougars together; these three being Jim, now an old dog, who dropped behind in a hard run, but still excellent on a cold trail; Tree'em, who, like Jim, had grown aged, but was very sure; and Bruno, who had become one of the best of all the pack on a hot trail, but who was apt to overrun it if it became at all difficult and cold. The biggest dog of the pack, a very powerful animal, was Badge, who was half foxhound and half what Johnny called Siberian bloodhound—I suppose a Great Dane or Ulm dog. His full brother Bill came next to him. There was a Rowdy in Jake's pack and another Rowdy in Johnny's, and each got badly hurt before the hunt was through. Jake's Rowdy, as soon as an animal was killed, became very cross and wished to attack any dog that came near. One of Jake's best hounds was old Bruise, a very sure, although not a particularly fast dog. All the members of the pack held the usual wild-beast attitude toward one another. They joined together for the chase and the fight, but once the quarry was killed, their relations among themselves became those of active hostility or selfish indifference. At feeding time each took whatever his strength permitted, and each paid abject deference to which-

Heading out for the hunt. T.R. is at far left.

ever animal was his known superior in prowess. Some of the younger dogs would now and then run deer or coyote. But the older dogs paid heed only to bear and bobcat; and the pack, as a body, discriminated sharply between the hounds they could trust and those which would go off on a wrong trail. The four terriers included a heavy, liver-colored half-breed bull-dog, a preposterous animal who looked as if his ancestry had included a toadfish. He was a terrible fighter, but his unvarying attitude toward mankind was one of effusive and rather foolish affection. In a fight he could whip any of the hounds save Badge, and he was far more willing than Badge to accept punishment. There was also a funny little black and tan, named Skip, a most friendly little fellow, especially fond of riding in front or behind the saddle of any one of us who would take him up, although perfectly able to travel forty miles a day on his own sturdy legs if he had to, and then to join in the worry of the quarry when once it had been shot. Porcupines abounded in the woods, and one or two of the terriers and half a dozen of the hounds positively refused to learn any wisdom, invariably attacking each porcupine they found; the result being that we had to spend many minutes in removing the quills from their mouths, eyes, etc. A white bull-terrier would come in from such a combat with his nose literally looking like a glorified pincushion, and many of the spines we had to take out with nippers. The terriers never ran with the hounds, but stayed behind with the horses until they heard the hounds barking "bayed" or "treed," when they forthwith tore toward them. Skip adopted me as his special master, rode with me whenever I would let him, and slept on the foot of my bed at night, growling defiance at anything that came near. I grew attached to the friendly, bright little fellow, and at the end of the hunt took him home with me as a playmate for the children.

It was a great, wild country. In the creek bottoms there were a good many ranches; but we only occasionally passed by these, on our way to our hunting grounds in the wilderness along the edge of the snow-line. The mountains crowded close together in chain, peak, and tableland; all the higher ones were wrapped in an unrent shroud of snow. We saw a good many deer, and fresh sign of elk, but no elk themselves, although we were informed that bands were to be found in the high spruce timber where the snows were so deep that it would have been impossible to go on horseback, while going on foot would have been inconceivably fatiguing. The country was open. The high peaks were bare of trees. Cottonwoods, and occasionally dwarfed birch or maple and willows, fringed the streams; aspens grew in groves higher up. There were pinyons and cedars on the slopes of the foothills; spruce clustered here and there in the cooler ravines and valleys and high up the mountains. The dense oak brush and thick growing cedars were hard on our clothes, and sometimes on our bodies.

Bear and cougars had once been very plentiful throughout this region, but during the last three or four years the cougars have greatly diminished in numbers throughout northern Colorado, and the bears have diminished also, although not to the same extent. The great grizzlies which were once fairly plentiful here are now very rare, as they are in most places in the United States. There remain plenty of the black and brown bears, which are simply individual color phases of the same species.

Bears are interesting creatures and their habits are always worth watching. When I used to hunt grizzlies my experience tended to make me lay special emphasis on their variation in temper. There are savage and cowardly bears, just as there are big and little ones; and sometimes these variations are very marked among bears of the same district, and at other times all the bears of one district will seem to have a common code of behavior which differs utterly from that of the bears of another district. Readers of Lewis and Clark do not need to be reminded of the great difference they found in ferocity between the bears of the upper Missouri and the bears of the Columbia River country; and those who have lived in the upper Missouri country nowadays know how widely the bears that still remain have altered in character from what they were as recently as the middle of the last century.

This variability has been shown in the bears which I have stumbled upon at close quarters. On but one occasion was I ever regularly charged by a grizzly. To this animal I had given a mortal wound, and without any effort at retaliation he bolted into a thicket of what, in my hurry, I thought was laurel (it being composed in reality, I suppose, of thick-growing berry bushes). On my following him and giving him a second wound, he charged very determinedly, taking two more bullets without flinching. I just escaped the charge by jumping to one side, and he died almost immediately after striking at me as he rushed by. This bear charged with his mouth open, but made very little noise after the growl or roar with which he greeted my second bullet. I mention the fact of his having kept his mouth open, because one or two of my friends who have been charged have informed me that in their cases they particularly noticed that the bear charged with his mouth shut. Perhaps the fact that my bear was shot through the lungs may account for the difference, or it may simply be another example of individual variation.

On another occasion, in a windfall, I got up within eight or ten feet of a grizzly, which simply bolted off, paying no heed to a hurried shot which I delivered as I poised unsteadily on the swaying top of an overthrown dead pine. On yet another occasion, when I roused a big bear from his sleep, he at the first moment seemed to pay little or no heed to me, and then turned toward me in a leisurely way, the only sign of hostility he betrayed being to ruffle up the hair on his shoulders and the back of his neck. I hit him square between the eyes, and he dropped like a pole-axed steer.

On another occasion I got up quite close to and mortally wounded a bear, which ran off without uttering a sound until it fell dead; but another of these grizzlies, which I shot from ambush, kept squalling and yelling every time I hit him, making a great rumpus. On one occasion one of my cowhands and myself were able to run down on foot a she grizzly bear and her cub, which had obtained a long start of us, simply because of the foolish conduct of the mother. The cub—or more properly the yearling, for it was a cub of the second year—ran on far ahead, and would have escaped if the old she had not continually stopped and sat up on her hind legs to look back at us. I think she did this partly from curiosity, but partly also from bad temper, for once or twice she grinned and roared at us. The upshot of it was that I got within range and put a bullet in the old she, who afterward charged my companion and was killed; and we also got the yearling.

One young grizzly which I killed many years ago dropped to the first bullet, which entered its stomach. It then let myself and my companion approach closely, looking up at us with alert curiosity, but making no effort to escape. It was really not crippled at all, but we thought from its actions that its back was broken, and my companion advanced to kill it with his pistol. The pistol, however, did not inflict a mortal wound, and the only effect was to make the young bear jump to its feet as if unhurt, and race off at full speed through the timber; for though not full grown it was beyond cubhood, being probably about eighteen months old. By desperate running I succeeded in getting another shot, and more by luck than by anything else knocked it over, this time permanently.

Black bear are not, under normal conditions, formidable brutes. If they do charge and get home they may maul a man severely, and there are a number of instances on record in which they have killed men. Ordinarily, however, a black bear will not charge home, though he may bluster a good deal. I once shot one very close up which made a most lamentable outcry, and seemed to lose its head, its efforts to escape resulting in its bouncing about among the trees with such heedless hurry that I was easily able to kill it. Another black bear, which I also shot at close quarters, came straight for my companions and myself, and almost ran over the white hunter who was with me. This bear made no sound whatever when I first hit it, and I do not think it was charging. I believe it was simply dazed, and by accident ran the wrong way, and so almost came into collision with us. However, when it found itself face to face with the white hunter, and only four or five feet away, it prepared for hostilities, and I think would have mauled him if I had not brained it with another bullet; for I was myself standing but six feet or so to one side of it. None of the bears shot on this Colorado trip made a sound when hit; they all died silently, like so many wolves.

Ordinarily, my experience has been that bears were not flurried when I suddenly came upon them. They impressed me as if they were always keeping in mind the place toward which they wished to retreat in the event of danger, and for this place, which was invariably a piece of rough ground or dense timber, they made off with all possible speed, not seeming to lose their heads.

Frequently I have been able to watch bears for some time while myself unobserved. With other game I have very often done this even when within close range, not wishing to kill creatures needlessly, or without a good object; but with bears, my experience has been that chances to secure them come so seldom as to make it very distinctly worth while improving any that do come, and I have not spent much time watching any bear unless he was in a place where I could not get at him, or else was so close at hand that I was not afraid of his getting away. On one occasion the bear was hard at work digging up squirrel or gopher *caches* on the side of a pine-clad hill; while at this work he looked rather like a big badger. On two other occasions the bear was fussing around a carcass preparatory to burying it. On these occasions I was very close, and it was extremely interesting to note the grotesque, half-human movements, and giant, awkward strength of the great beast. He would twist the carcass around with the utmost ease, sometimes taking it in his teeth and dragging it, at other times grasping it in his forepaws and half lifting, half shoving it. Once the bear lost his grip and rolled over during the course of some movement, and this made him angry, and he struck the carcass a savage whack, just as a pettish child will strike a table against which it has knocked itself. At another time I watched a black bear some distance off getting his breakfast under stumps and stones. He was very active, turning the stone or log over, and then thrusting his muzzle into the empty space to gobble up the small creatures below before they recovered from their surprise and the sudden inflow of light. From under one log he put a chipmunk, and danced hither and thither with even more agility than awkwardness, slapping at the chipmunk with his paw while it zigzagged about, until finally he scooped it into his mouth.

All this was in the old days when I was still-hunting, with only the rifle. This Colorado trip was the first on which I hunted bears with hounds. If we had run across a grizzly there would doubtless have been a chance to show some prowess, at least in the way of hard riding. But the black and brown bears cannot, save under exceptional circumstances, escape from such a pack as we had with us; and the real merit of the chase was confined to the hounds and to Jake and Johnny for their skill in handling them. Perhaps I should add the horses, for their extraordinary endurance and surefootedness. As for the rest of us, we needed to do little more than to sit ten or twelve hours in the saddle and occasionally lead the horses up or down the most precipitous and cliff-like of the mountain sides. But it was great fun, nevertheless, and usually a chase lasted long enough to be interesting.

The first day after reaching camp we rode for eleven hours over a very difficult country, but without getting above the snow-line. Finally the dogs got on the fresh trail of a bobcat, and away they went. A bobcat will often give a good run, much better, on the average, than a cougar; and this one puzzled the dogs not a little at first. It scrambled out of one deep valley, crossing and recrossing the rock ledges where its scent was hard to follow; then plunged into another valley. Meanwhile we had ridden up on the high mountain spur between the two valleys, and after scrambling and galloping to and fro as the cry veered from point to point when the dogs changed directions, we saw them cross into the second valley. Here again they took a good deal of time to puzzle out the trail, and became somewhat scattered. We had dismounted and were standing by the horses' heads, listening to the baying and trying to decide which way we should go, when Stewart suddenly pointed us out a bear. It was on the other side of the valley from us, and perhaps half a mile away, galloping down hill, with two of the hounds after it, and in the sunlight its fur looked glossy black. In a minute or two it passed out of sight in the thick-growing timber at the bottom of the valley; and as we afterward found, the two hounds, getting momentarily thrown out, and hearing the others still baying on the cat trail, joined the latter. Jake started off to go around the head of the valley, while the rest of us plunged down into it. We found from the track that the bear had gone up the valley, and Jake found where he had come out on the high divide, and then turned and retraced his steps. But the hounds were evidently all after the cat. There was nothing for us to do but follow them. Sometimes riding, sometimes leading the horses, we went up the steep hillside, and as soon as we reached the crest heard the hounds barking treed. Shorty and Skip, who always trotted after the horses while the hounds were in full cry on a trail, recognized the change of note immediately, and tore off in the direction of the bay, while we followed as best we could, hoping to get there in time for Stewart and Lambert to take photographs of the lynx in a tree. But we were too late. Both Shorty and Skip could climb trees, and although Skip was too light to tackle a bobcat by himself, Shorty, a heavy, formidable dog, of unflinching courage and great physical strength, was altogether too much for any bobcat. When we reached the place we found the bobcat in the top of a pinyon, and Shorty steadily working his way up through the branches and very near the quarry. Evidently the bobcat felt that the situation needed the taking of desperate chances, and just before Shorty reached it out it jumped, Shorty yelling with excitement as he plunged down through the branches after it. But the cat did not jump far enough. One of the hounds seized it by the hind leg and in another second everything was over.

Shorty was always the first of the pack to attack dangerous game, and in attacking bear or cougar even Badge was much less reckless and more wary. In consequence, Shorty was seamed over with scars; most of them from bobcats, but one or two from cougars. He could speedily kill a bobcat single-handed; for these small lynxes are not really formidable fighters, although they will lacerate a dog quite severely. Shorty found a badger a much more difficult antagonist than a bobcat. A bobcat in a hole makes a hard fight, however. On this hunt we once got a bobcat under a big rock, and Jake's Rowdy in trying to reach it got so badly mauled that he had to join the invalid class for several days.

The bobcat we killed this first day was a male, weighing twenty-five pounds. It was too late to try after the bear, especially as we had only ten or a dozen dogs out, while the bear's tracks showed it to be a big one; and we rode back to camp.

Next morning we rode off early, taking with us all twenty-six hounds and the four terriers. We wished first to find whether the bear had gone out of the country in which we had seen him, and so rode up a valley and then scrambled laboriously up the mountain-side to the top of the snow-covered divide. Here the snow was three feet deep in places, and the horses plunged and floundered as we worked our way in single file through the drifts. But it had frozen hard the previous night, so that a bear could walk on the crust and leave very little sign. In consequence we came near passing over the place where the animal we were after had actually crossed out of the canyon-like ravine in which we had seen him and gone over the divide into another set of valleys.

Bear hunters.

The trail was so faint that it puzzled us, as we could not be certain how fresh it was, and until this point could be cleared up we tried to keep the hounds from following it. Old Jim, however, slipped off to one side and speedily satisfied himself that the trail was fresh. Along it he went, giving tongue, and the other dogs were maddened by the sound, while Jim, under such circumstances, paid no heed whatever to any effort to make him come back. Accordingly, the other hounds were slipped after him, and down they ran into the valley, while we slid, floundered, and scrambled along the ridge crest parallel to them, until a couple of miles farther on we worked our way down to some great slopes covered with dwarf scrub-oak. At the edge of these slopes, where they fell off in abrupt descent to the stream at the bottom of the valley, we halted. Opposite us was a high and very rugged mountain-side covered with a growth of pinyon—never a close-growing tree—its precipitous flanks broken by ledges and scored by gullies and ravines. It was hard to follow the scent across such a mountain-side, and the dogs speedily became much scattered. We could hear them plainly, and now and then could see them, looking like ants as they ran up and down hill and along the ledges. Finally we heard some of them barking bayed. The volume of sound increased steadily as the straggling dogs joined those which had first reached the hunted animal. At about this time, to our astonishment, Badge, usually a staunch fighter, rejoined us, followed by one or two other hounds, who seemed to have had enough of the matter. Immediately afterward we saw the bear, half-way up the opposite mountainside. The hounds were all around him, and occasionally bit at his hind quarters; but he had evidently no intention of climbing a tree. When we first saw him he was sitting up on a point of rock surrounded by the pack, his black fur showing to fine advantage. Then he moved off, threatening the dogs, and making what in Mississippi is called a walking bay. He was a sullen, powerful beast, and his leisurely gait showed how little he feared the pack, and how confident he was in his own burly strength. By this time the dogs had been after him for a couple of hours, and as there was no water on the mountain-side we feared they might be getting exhausted, and rode toward them as rapidly as we could. It was a hard climb up to where they were, and we had to lead the horses. Just as we came in sight of him, across a deep gully which ran down the sheer mountain-side, he broke bay and started off, threatening the foremost of the pack as they dared to approach him. They were all around him, and for a minute I could not fire; then as he passed under a pinyon I got a clear view of his great round stern and pulled trigger. The bullet broke both his hips, and he rolled down hill, the hounds yelling with excitement as they closed in on him. He could still play havoc with the pack, and there was need to kill him at once. I leaped and slid down on my side of the gully as he rolled down his; at the bottom he stopped and raised himself on his fore quarters; and with another bullet I broke his back between the shoulders.

Immediately all the dogs began to worry the carcass, while their savage baying echoed so loudly in the narrow, steep gully that we could with difficulty hear one another speak. It was a wild scene to look upon, as we scrambled down to where the dead bear lay on his back between the rocks. He did not die wholly unavenged, for he had killed one of the terriers and six other dogs were more or less injured. The chase of the bear is grim work for the pack. Jim, usually a very wary fighter, had a couple of deep holes in his thigh; but the most mishandled of the wounded dogs was Shorty. With his usual dauntless courage he had gone straight at the bear's head. Being such a heavy, powerful animal, I think if he had been backed up he could have held the bear's head down, and prevented the beast from doing much injury. As it was, the bear bit through the side of Shorty's head, and bit him in the shoulder, and again in the hip, inflicting very bad wounds. Once the fight was over Shorty lay down on the hillside, unable to move. When we started home we put him beside a little brook, and left a piece of bear meat by him, as it was obvious we could not get him to camp that day. Next day one of the boys went back with a pack-horse to take him in; but half-way out met him struggling toward camp, and returned. Late in the afternoon Shorty turned up while we were at dinner, and staggered toward us, wagging his tail with enthusiastic delight at seeing his friends. We fed him until he could not hold another mouthful; then he curled up in a dry corner of the cook-tent and slept for forty-eight hours; and two or three days afterward was able once more to go hunting.

The bear was a big male, weighing three hundred and thirty pounds. On examination at close quarters, his fur, which was in fine condition, was not as black as it had seemed when seen afar off, the roots of the hairs being brown. There was nothing whatever in his stomach. Evidently he had not yet begun to eat, and had been but a short while out of his hole. Bear feed very little when they first come out of their dens, sometimes beginning on grass, sometimes on buds. Occasionally they will feed at carcasses and try to kill animals within a week or two after they have left winter quarters, but this is rare, and as a usual thing for the first few weeks after they have come out they feed much as a deer would. Although not hog fat, as would probably have been the case in the fall, this bear was in good condition. In the fall, however, he would doubtless have weighed over four hundred pounds. The three old females we got on this trip weighed one hundred and eighty, one hundred and seventy-five, and one hundred and thirty-five pounds apiece. The yearlings weighed from thirty-one to forty pounds. The only other black bears I ever weighed all belonged to the sub-species *Luteolus*, and were killed on the Little Sunflower River, in Mississippi, in the late fall of nineteen hundred and two. A big old male, in poor condition, weighed two hundred and eighty-five pounds, and two very fat females weighed two hundred and twenty and two hundred and thirty-five pounds respectively.

The next few days we spent in hunting perseveringly, but unsuccessfully. Each day we were from six to twelve hours in the saddle, climbing with weary toil up the mountains and slipping and scrambling down them. On the tops and on the north slopes there was much snow, so that we had to pick our trails carefully, and even thus the horses often floundered belly-deep as we worked along in single file; the men on the horses which were best at snow bucking took turns in breaking the trail. In the worst places we had to dismount and lead the horses, often over such bad ground that nothing less sure-footed than the tough mountain ponies could even have kept their legs. The weather was cold, with occasional sharp flurries of snow, and once a regular snowstorm. We found the tracks of one or two bears, but in each case several days old, and it was evident either that the bears had gone back to their dens, finding the season so late, or else that they were lying quiet in sheltered places, and travelling as little as possible. One day, after a long run of certainly five or six miles through very difficult country, the dogs treed a bobcat in a big cedar. It had run so far that it was badly out of breath. Stewart climbed the tree and took several photographs of it, pushing the camera up to within about four feet of where the cat sat. Lambert obtained photographs of both Stewart and the cat. Shorty was at this time still an invalid from his encounter with the bear, but Skip worked his way thirty feet up the tree in his effort to get at the bobcat. Lambert shot the latter with his revolver, the bobcat dying stuck in the branches; and he then had to climb the tree to get both the bobcat and Skip, as the latter was at such a height that we thought he would hurt himself if he fell. Another bobcat when treed sealed his own fate by stepping on a dead branch and falling right into the jaws of the pack.

At this camp, as everywhere, the tiny four-striped chipmunks were plentiful and tame; they are cheerful, attractive little animals. We also saw white-footed mice and a big meadow mouse around camp; and we found a young brushy-tailed pack-rat. The snowshoe rabbits were still white on the mountains, but in the lower valleys they had changed to the summer pelage. On the mountains we occasionally saw woodchucks and rock squirrels of two kinds, a large and a small—*Spermophilus grammurus* and *armatus*. The noisy, cheerful pine squirrels were common where the woods were thick. There were eagles and ravens in the mountains, and once we saw sandhill cranes soaring far above the highest peaks. The long-crested jays came familiarly around camp, but on this occasion we only saw the whiskey-jacks, Clark's nutcrackers and magpies, while off in the mountains. Among the pinyons, we several times came across straggling flocks of the queer pinyon jays or blue crows, with their unmistakable calls and almost blackbird-like habits. There were hawks of several species, and blue grouse, while the smaller birds included flickers, robins, and the beautiful mountain bluebirds. Juncos and mountain chickadees were plentiful, and the ruby-crowned kinglets were singing with astonishing power for such tiny birds. We came on two nests of the red-tailed hawk; the birds were brooding, and seemed tame and unwary.

After a week of this we came to the conclusion that the snow was too deep and the weather too cold for us to expect to get any more bear in the immediate neighborhood, and accordingly shifted camp to where Clear Creek joins West Divide Creek.

The first day's hunt from the new camp was successful. We were absent about eleven hours and rode some forty miles. The day included four hours' steady snow bucking, for the bear, as soon as they got the chance, went through the thick timber where the snow lay deepest. Some two hours after leaving camp we found the old tracks of a she and a yearling, but it took us a much longer time before we finally struck the fresh trail made late the previous night or early in the morning. It was Jake who first found this fresh track, while Johnny with the pack was a couple of miles away, slowly but surely puzzling out the cold trail and keeping the dogs up to their work. As soon as Johnny came up we put all the hounds on the tracks, and away they went, through and over the snow, yelling their eager delight. Meanwhile we had fixed our saddles and were ready for what lay ahead. It was wholly impossible to ride at the tail of the pack, but we did our best to keep within sound of the baying. Finally, after much hard work and much point riding through snow, slush, and deep mud, on the level, and along, up, and down sheer slopes, we heard the dogs barking treed in the middle of a great grove of aspens high up the mountainside. The snow was too deep for the horses, and leaving them, we trudged heavily up on foot. The yearling was in the top of a tall aspen. Lambert shot it with his rifle and we then put the dogs on the trail of the old she. Some of the young ones did not know what to make of this, evidently feeling that the tracks must be those of the bear that they had already killed; but the veterans were in fully cry at once. We scrambled after them up the steep mountain, and then downward along ridges and spurs, getting all the clear ground we could. Finally we had to take to the snow, and floundered and slid through the drifts until we were in the valley. Most of the time the dogs were within hearing, giving tongue

The president and his quarry.

as they followed the trail. Finally a total change in the note showed that they were barking treed; and as rapidly as possible we made our way toward the sound. Again we found ourselves unable to bring the horses up to where the bear had treed, and scrambled thither on foot through the deep snow.

The bear was some thirty or forty feet up a tall spruce; it was a big she, with a glossy black-brown coat. I was afraid that at our approach she might come down; but she had been running hard for some four hours, had been pressed close, and evidently had not the slightest idea of putting herself of her own free will within the reach of the pack, which was now frantically baying at the foot of the tree. I shot her through the heart. As the bullet struck she climbed up through the branches with great agility for six or eight feet; then her muscles relaxed, and down she came with a thud, nearly burying herself in the snow. Little Skip was one of the first dogs to seize her as she came down; and in another moment he literally disappeared under the hounds as they piled on the bear. As soon as possible we got off the skin and pushed campward at a good gait, for we were a long way off. Just at nightfall we came out on a bluff from which we could overlook the rushing, swirling brown torrent, on the farther bank of which the tents were pitched.

The stomach of this bear contained nothing but buds. Like the other shes killed on this trip, she was accompanied by her yearling young, but had no newly born cub; sometimes bear breed only every other year, but I have found the mother accompanied not only by her cub but by her young of the year before. The yearling also had nothing but buds in its stomach. When its skin was taken off, Stewart looked at it, shook his head, and turning to Lambert said solemnly, "Alex., that skin isn't big enough to use for anything but a doily." From that time until the end of the hunt the yearlings were only known as "doily bears."

Next morning we again went out, and this time for twelve hours steadily, in the saddle, and now and then on foot. Most of the time we were in snow, and it was extraordinary that the horses could get through it at all, especially in working up the steep mountain-sides. But until it got so deep that they actually floundered—that is, so long as they could get their legs down to the bottom—I found that they could travel much faster than I could. On this day some twenty good-natured, hard-riding young fellows from the ranches within a radius of a dozen miles had joined our party to "see the President kill a bear." They were a cheerful and eagerly friendly crowd, as hardy as so many young moose, and utterly fearless horsemen; one of them rode his wild, nervous horse bareback, because it had bucked so when he tried to put the saddle on it that morning that he feared he would get left behind, and so abandoned the saddle outright. Whenever they had a chance they all rode at headlong speed, paying no heed to the slope of the mountainside or the character of the ground. In the deep snow they did me a real service, for of course they had to ride their horses single file through the drifts, and by the time my turn came we had a good trail.

After a good deal of beating to and fro, we found where an old she-bear with two yearlings had crossed a hill during the night and put the hounds on their tracks. Johnny and Jake, with one or two of the cowboys, followed the hounds over the exceedingly difficult hillside where the trail led; or rather, they tried to follow them, for the hounds speedily got clear away, as there were many places where they could run on the crust of the snow, in which the horses wallowed almost helpless. The rest of us went down to the valley, where the snow was light and the going easier. The bear had travelled hither and thither through the woods on the sidehill, and the dogs became scattered. Moreover, they jumped several deer, and four or five of the young dogs took after one of the latter. Finally, however, the rest of the pack put up the three bears. We had an interesting glimpse of the chase as the bears quartered up across an open spot of the hillside. The hounds were but a short distance behind them, strung out in a long string, the more powerful, those which could do best in the snow-bucking, taking the lead. We pushed up the mountain-side after them, horse after horse getting down in the snow, and speedily heard the redoubled clamor which told us that something had been treed. It was half an hour before we could make our way to the tree, a spruce, in which the two yearlings had taken refuge, while around the bottom the entire pack was gathered, crazy with excitement. We could not take the yearlings alive, both because we lacked the means of carrying them, and because we were anxious to get after the old bear. We could not leave them where they were, because it would have been well-nigh impossible to get the dogs away, and because, even if we had succeeded in getting them away, they would not have run any other trail as long as they knew the yearlings were in the tree. It was therefore out of the question to leave them unharmed, as we should have been glad to do, and Lambert killed them both with his revolver; the one that was first hit immediately began biting its brother. The ranchmen took them home to eat.

The hounds were immediately put on the trail of the old one and disappeared over the snow. In a few minutes we followed. It was heavy work getting up the mountainside through the drifts, but once on top we made our way down a nearly bare spur, and then turned to the right, scrambled a couple of miles along a slippery sidehill, and halted. Below us lay a great valley, on the farther side of which a spruce forest stretched up toward the treeless peaks. Snow covered even the bottom of the valley, and lay deep and solid in the spruce forest on the mountain-side. The hounds were in full cry, evidently on a hot trail, and we caught glimpses of them far on the opposite side of the valley, crossing little open glades in the spruce timber. If the crust was hard they scattered out. Where it was at all soft they ran in single file. We worked our way down toward them, and on reaching the bottom of the valley, went up it as fast as the snow would allow. Finally we heard the pack again barking treed and started toward them. They had treed the bear far up the mountain-side in the thick spruce timber, and a short experiment showed us that the horses could not possibly get through the snow. Accordingly, off we jumped and went toward the sound on foot, all the young ranchmen and cowboys rushing ahead, and thereby again making me an easy trail. On the way to the tree the rider of the bareback horse pounced on a snowshoe rabbit which was crouched under a bush and caught it with his hands. It was half an hour before we reached the tree, a big spruce, up which the bear had gone to a height of some forty feet. I broke her neck with a single bullet. She was smaller than the one I had shot the day before, but full grown. In her stomach, as in those of the two yearlings, there were buds of rose-bushes and quaking aspens. One yearling had also swallowed a mouse. It was a long ride to camp, and darkness had fallen by the time we caught the gleam from the lighted tents, across the dark stream.

With neither of these last two bear had there been any call for prowess; my part was merely to kill the bear dead at the first shot, for the sake of the pack. But the days were very enjoyable, nevertheless. It was good fun to be twelve hours in the saddle in such wild and beautiful country, to look at and listen to the hounds as they worked, and finally to see the bear treed and looking down at the maddened pack baying beneath.

For the next two or three days I was kept in camp by a touch of

Cuban fever. On one of these days Lambert enjoyed the longest hunt we had on the trip, after an old she-bear and three yearlings. The yearlings treed one by one, each of course necessitating a stoppage, and it was seven in the evening before the old bear at last went up a cottonwood and was shot; she was only wounded, however, and in the fight she crippled Johnny's Rowdy before she was killed. When the hunters reached camp it was thirteen hours since they had left it. The old bear was a very light brown; the first yearling was reddish-brown, the second light yellowish-brown, the third dark black-brown, though all were evidently of the same litter.

Following this came a spell of bad weather, snowstorm and blizzard steadily succeeding one another. This lasted until my holiday was over. Some days we had to stay in camp. On other days we hunted; but there was three feet of new snow on the summits and foothills, making it difficult to get about. We saw no more bear, and, indeed, no more beartracks that were less than two or three weeks old.

We killed a couple of bobcats. The chase of one was marked by several incidents. We had been riding through a blizzard on the top of a plateau, and were glad to plunge down into a steep sheer-sided valley. By the time we reached the bottom there was a lull in the storm and we worked our way with considerable difficulty through the snow, down timber, and lava rock, toward Divide Creek. After a while the valley widened a little, spruce and aspens fringing the stream at the bottom while the sides were bare. Here we struck a fresh bobcat trail leading off up one of the mountain-sides. The hounds followed it nearly to the top, then turned and came down again, worked through the timber in the bottom, and struck out on the hillside opposite. Suddenly we saw the bobcat running ahead of them and doubling and circling. A few minutes afterward the hounds followed the trail to the creek bottom and then began to bark treed. But on reaching the point we found there was no cat in the tree, although the dogs seemed certain that there was; and Johnny and Jake speedily had them again running on the trail. After making its way for some distance through the bottom, the cat had again taken to the sidehill, and the hounds went after it hard. Again they went nearly to the top, again they streamed down to the bottom and crossed the creek. Soon afterward we saw the cat ahead of them. For the moment it threw them off the track by making a circle and galloping around close to the rearmost hounds. It then made for the creek bottom, where it climbed to the top of a tall aspen. The hounds soon picked up the trail again, and followed it full cry; but unfortunately just before they reached where it had treed they ran on to a porcupine. When we reached the foot of the aspen, in the top of which the bobcat crouched, with most of the pack baying beneath, we found the porcupine dead and half a dozen dogs with their muzzles and throats filled full of quills. Before doing anything with the cat it was necessary to take these quills out. One of the terriers, which always found porcupines an irresistible attraction, was a really extraordinary sight, so thickly were the quills studded over his face and chest. But a big hound was in even worse condition; the quills were stuck in abundance into his nose, lips, cheeks, and tongue, and in the roof of his mouth they were almost as thick as bristles in a brush. Only by use of pincers was it possible to rid these two dogs of the quills, and it was a long and bloody job. The others had suffered less.

The dogs seemed to have no sympathy with one another, and apparently all that the rest of the pack felt was that they were kept a long time waiting for the cat. They never stopped baying for a minute, and Shorty, as was his habit, deliberately bit great patches of bark from the aspens, to show his impatience; for the tree in which the cat stood was not one which he could climb. After attending to the porcupine dogs one of the men climbed the tree and with a stick pushed out the cat. It dropped down through the branches forty or fifty feet, but was so quick in starting and dodging that it actually rushed through the pack, crossed the stream, and, doubling and twisting, was off up the creek through the timber. It ran cunning, and in a minute or two lay down under a bush and watched the hounds as they went by, overrunning its trail. Then it took off up the hillside; but the hounds speedily picked up its track, and running in single file, were almost on it. Then the cat turned down hill, but too late, for it was overtaken within fifty yards. This ended our hunting.

On Sunday we rode down some six miles from camp to a little blue school-house and attended service. The preacher was in the habit of riding over every alternate Sunday from Rifle, a little town twenty or twenty-five miles away; and the ranchmen with their wives and children, some on horseback, some in wagons, had gathered from thirty miles round to attend the service. The crowd was so large that the exercises had to take place in the open air, and it was pleasant to look at the strong frames and rugged, weather-beaten faces of the men; while as for the women, one respected them even more than the men.

In spite of the snowstorms spring was coming; some of the trees were beginning to bud and show green, more and more flowers were in bloom, and bird life was steadily increasing. In the bushes by the streams the handsome white-crowned sparrows and green-tailed towhees were in full song, making attractive music; although the song of neither can rightly be compared in point of plaintive beauty with that of the white-throated sparrow, which, except some of the thrushes, and perhaps the winter wren, is the sweetest singer of the Northeastern forests. The spurred towhees were very plentiful; and one morning a willow-thrush sang among the willows like a veery. Both the crested jays and the Woodhouse jays came around camp. Lower down the Western meadow larks were singing beautifully, and vesper finches were abundant. Say's flycatcher, a very attractive bird, with pretty, soft-colored plumage, continually uttering a plaintive single note, and sometimes a warbling twitter, flitted about in the neighborhood of the little log ranch houses. Gangs of blackbirds visited the corrals. I saw but one song sparrow, and curiously enough, though I think it was merely an individual peculiarity, this particular bird had a song entirely different from any I have heard from the familiar Eastern bird—always a favorite of mine.

While up in the mountains hunting, we twice came upon owls, which were rearing their families in the deserted nests of the red-tailed hawk. One was a long-eared owl, and the other a great horned owl, of the pale Western variety. Both were astonishingly tame, and we found it difficult to make them leave their nests, which were in the tops of cottonwood trees.

On the last day we rode down to where Glenwood Springs lies, hemmed in by lofty mountain chains, which are riven in sunder by sheer-sided, cliff-walled canyons. As we left ever farther behind us the wintry desolation of our high hunting grounds we rode into full spring. The green of the valley was a delight to the eye; bird songs sounded on every side, from the fields and from the trees and bushes beside the brooks and irrigation ditches; the air was sweet with the spring-time breath of many budding things. The sarvice bushes were white with bloom, like shad-blow on the Hudson; the blossoms of the Oregon grape made yellow mats on the ground. We saw the chunky Say's ground squirrel, looking like a big chipmunk, with on each side a conspicuous white stripe edged with black. In one place we saw quite a large squirrel, grayish, with red on the lower back. I suppose it was only a pine squirrel, but it looked like one of the gray squirrels of southern Colorado.

Mountain mockers and the handsome, bold Arkansaw king birds were numerous. The black-tail sage sparrow was conspicuous in the sagebrush, and high among the cliffs the white-throated swifts were soaring. There were numerous warblers, among which I could only make out the black-throated gray, Audubon's, and McGillivray's. In Glenwood Springs itself the purple finches, house finches, and Bullock's orioles were in full song. Flocks of siskins passed with dipping flight. In one rapid little stream we saw a water ousel. Hummingbirds—I suppose the broad-tailed—were common, and as they flew they made, intermittently and almost rhythmically, a curious metallic sound; seemingly it was done with their wings.

But the thing that interested me most in the way of bird life was something I saw in Denver. To my delight I found that the huge hotel at which we took dinner was monopolized by the pretty, musical house finches, to the exclusion of the ordinary city sparrows. The latter are all too plentiful in Denver, as in every other city, and, as always, are noisy, quarrelsome—in short, thoroughly unattractive and disreputable. The house finch, on the contrary, is attractive in looks, in song, and in ways. It was delightful to hear the males singing, often on the wing. They went right up to the top stories of the high hotel, and nested under the eaves and in the cornices. The cities of the Southwestern states are to be congratulated on having this spirited, attractive little songster as a familiar dweller around their houses and in their gardens.

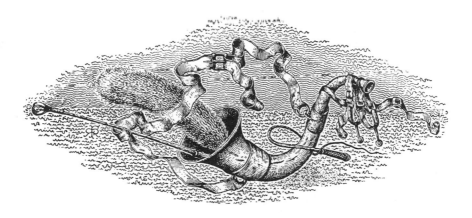

ZANE GREY.

1918

Zane Grey is perhaps the best known of all of our Western writers, and even today—some forty years after his death—many of his eighty-nine books remain in print. Such popular successes as *Riders of the Purple Sage* prompted the creation of the "Zane Grey Theater" in the 1950s, one of television's first Westerns.

Grey was, of course, hardly aloof from his subject, the West, and he was particularly fond of hunting and fishing in the Rocky Mountains. Many of his non-fiction books—including *Tales of Lonely Trails*, from which the following selection was taken—were chronicles of these adventures, and prove to be at least as captivating as his novels. Such essays as "Colorado Trails" also reveal a tremendously thoughtful man, who, as if to offset the triviality of his novels, emerges as an individual sensitive to his place in nature. Grey was not afraid to question the "sport" in "sportsmanship," and in this essay he wonders aloud about the nobility of hunting. It is ironic to note that Grey's deepest misgivings about the hunt are brought out in the description of the pursuit of a grizzly bear—a species that is now all but extinct in Colorado.

COLORADO TRAILS

RIDING AND TRAMPING trails would lose half their charm if the motive were only to hunt and to fish. It seems fair to warn the reader who longs to embark upon a bloody game hunt or a chronicle of fishing records that this is not that kind of story. But it will be one for those who love horses and dogs, the long winding dim trails, the wild flowers and the dark still woods, the fragrance of spruce and the smell of camp-fire smoke. And as well for those who love to angle in brown lakes or rushing brooks or chase after the baying hounds or stalk the stag on his lonely heights.

We left Denver on August twenty-second over the Moffet road and had a long wonderful ride through the mountains. The Rockies have a sweep, a limitless sweep, majestic and grand. For many miles we crossed no streams, and climbed and wound up barren slopes. Once across the divide, however, we descended into a country of black forests and green valleys. Yampa, a little hamlet with a past prosperity, lay in the wide valley of the Bear River. It was picturesque but idle, and a better name for it would have been Sleepy Hollow. The main and only street was very wide and dusty, bordered by old board walks and vacant stores. It seemed a deserted street of a deserted village. Teague, the guide, lived there. He assured me it was not quite as lively a place as in the early days when it was a stage center for an old and rich mining section. We stayed there at the one hotel for a whole day, most of which I spent sitting on the board walk. Whenever I chanced to look down the wide street it seemed always the same—deserted. But Yampa had the charm of being old and forgotten, and for that reason I would like to live there a while.

Reprinted by permission of Zane Grey, Inc.

On August twenty-third we started in two buckboards for the foot-hills, some fifteen miles westward, where Teague's men were to meet us with saddle and pack horses. The ride was not interesting until the Flattop Mountains began to loom, and we saw the dark green slopes of spruce, rising to bare gray cliffs and domes, spotted with white banks of snow. I felt the first cool breath of mountain air, exhilarating and sweet. From that moment I began to live.

We had left at six-thirty. Teague, my guide, had been so rushed with his manifold tasks that I had scarcely seen him, let alone gotten acquainted with him. And on this ride he was far behind with our load of baggage. We arrived at the edge of the foothills about noon. It appeared to be the gateway of a valley, with aspen groves and ragged jack-pines on the slopes, and a stream running down. Our driver called it the Still-water. That struck me as strange, for the stream was in a great hurry. R. C. spied trout in it, and schools of darkish, mullet-like fish which we were informed were grayling. We wished for our tackle then and for time to fish.

Teague's man, a young fellow called Virgil, met us here. He did not resemble the ancient Virgil in the least, but he did look as if he had walked right out of one of my romances of wild riders. So I took a liking to him at once.

But the bunch of horses he had corralled there did not excite any delight in me. Horses, of course, were the most important part of our outfit. And that moment of first seeing the horses that were to carry us on such long rides was an anxious and thrilling one. I have felt it many times, and it never grows any weaker from experience. Many a scrubby lot of horses had turned out well upon acquaintance, and some I had found hard to part with at the end of trips. Up to that time, however, I had not seen a bear hunter's horses; and I was much con-cerned by the fact that these were a sorry looking outfit, dusty, ragged, maneless, cut and bruised and crippled. Still, I reflected, they were bunched up so closely that I could not tell much about them, and I decided to wait for Teague before I chose a horse for any one.

In an hour Teague trotted up to our resting place. Beside his own mount he had two white saddle horses, and nine pack-animals, heavily laden. Teague was a sturdy rugged man with bronzed face and keen gray-blue eyes, very genial and humorous. Straightway I got the impres-sion that he liked work.

"Let's organize," he said, briskly. "Have you picked the horses you're goin' to ride?"

Teague led from the midst of that dusty kicking bunch a rangy powerful horse, with four white feet, a white face and a noble head. He had escaped my eye. I felt thrillingly that here at least was one horse.

The rest of the horses were permanently crippled or temporarily lame, and I had no choice, except to take the one it would be kindest to ride.

"He ain't much like your Silvermane or Black Star," said Teague, laughing.

"What do you know about them?" I asked, very much pleased at this from him.

"Well, I know all about them," he replied. "I'll have you the best horse in this country in a few days. Fact is I've bought him, an' he'll come with my cowboy, Vern. . . . Now, we're organized. Let's move."

We rode through a meadow along a spruce slope above which towered the great mountain. It was a zigzag trail, rough, boggy, and steep in places. The Stillwater meandered here, and little breaks on the water gave evidence of feeding trout. We had several miles of meadow, and then sheered off to the left up into the timber. It was a spruce forest, very still and fragrant. We climbed out up on a bench, and across a flat, up another bench, out of the timber into the patches of snow. Here snow could be felt in the air. Water was everywhere. I saw a fox, a badger, and another furry creature, too illusive to name. One more climb brought us to the top of the Flattop Pass, about eleven thousand feet. The view in the direction from which we had come was splendid, and led the eye to the distant sweeping ranges, dark and dim along the horizon. The Flattops were flat enough, but not very wide at this pass, and we were soon going down again into a green gulf of spruce, with ragged peaks lifting beyond. Here again I got the suggestion of limitless space. It took us an hour to ride down to Little Trappers Lake, a small clear green sheet of water. The larger lake was farther down. It was big, irregular, and bordered by spruce forests, and shadowed by the lofty gray peaks.

The Camp was on the far side. The air appeared rather warm, and mosquitoes bothered us. However, they did not stay long. It was after sunset and I was too tired to have many impressions.

Our cook appeared to be a melancholy man. He had a deep quavering voice, a long drooping mustache and sad eyes. He was silent

Trapper's Lake.

most of the time. The men called him Bill, and yelled when they spoke, for he was somewhat deaf. It did not take me long to discover that he was a good cook.

Our tent was pitched down the slope from the cook tent. We were too tired to sit round a camp-fire and talk. The stars were white and splendid, and they hung over the flat ridges like great beacon lights. The lake appeared to be inclosed on three sides by amphitheatric mountains, black with spruce up to the gray walls of rock. The night grew cold and very still. The bells on the horses tinkled distantly. There was a soft murmur of falling water. A lonesome coyote barked, and that thrilled me. Teague's dogs answered this prowler, and some of them had voices to make a hunter thrill. One, the bloodhound Cain, had a roar like a lion's. I had not gotten acquainted with the hounds, and I was thinking about them when I fell asleep.

Next morning I was up at five-thirty. The air was cold and nipping and frost shone on grass and sage. A red glow of sunrise gleamed on the tip of the mountain and slowly grew downward.

The cool handle of an axe felt good. I soon found, however, that I could not wield it long for lack of breath. The elevation was close to ten thousand feet and the air at that height was thin and rare. After each series of lusty strokes I had to rest. R. C., who could handle an axe as he used to swing a baseball bat, made fun of my efforts. Whereupon I relinquished the tool to him, and chuckled at his discomfiture.

After breakfast R. C. and I got out our tackles and rigged up fly rods, and sallied forth to the lake with the same eagerness we had felt when we were boys going after chubs and sunfish. The lake glistened green in the sunlight and it lay like a gem at the foot of the magnificent black slopes.

The water was full of little floating particles that Teague called wild rice. I thought the lake had begun to work, like eastern lakes during dog days. It did not look propitious for fishing, but Teague reassured us. The outlet of this lake was the head of White River. We tried the outlet first, but trout were not rising there. Then we began wading and casting along a shallow bar of the lake. Teague had instructed us to cast, then drag the flies slowly across the surface of the water, in imitation of a swimming fly or bug. I tried this, and several times, when the leader was close to me and my rod far back, I had strikes. With my rod in that position I could not hook the trout. Then I cast my own way, letting the flies sink a little. To my surprise and dismay I had only a few strikes and could not hook the fish.

R. C., however, had better luck, and that too in wading right over the ground I had covered. To beat me at anything always gave him the most unaccountable fiendish pleasure.

"These are educated trout," he said. "It takes a skillful fisherman to make them rise. Now anybody can catch the big game of the sea, which is your forte. But here you are N. G. . . . Watch me cast!"

I watched him make a most atrocious cast. But the water boiled, and he hooked two good-sized trout at once. Quite speechless with envy and admiration I watched him play them and eventually beach them. They were cutthroat trout, silvery-sided and marked with the red slash along their gills that gave them their name. I did not catch any while wading, but from the bank I spied one, and dropping a fly in front of his nose, I got him. R. C. caught four more, all about a pound in weight, and then he had a strike that broke his leader. He did not have another leader, so we walked back to camp.

Wild flowers colored the open slopes leading down out of the forest.

Golden rod, golden daisies, and bluebells were plentiful and very pretty. Here I found my first columbine, the beautiful flower that is the emblem of Colorado. In vivid contrast to its blue, Indian paint brush thinly dotted the slopes and varied in color from red to pink and from white to yellow.

My favorite of all wild flowers—the purple asters—were there too, on tall nodding stems, with pale faces held up to the light. The reflection of mountain and forest in Trappers Lake was clear and beautiful.

The hounds bayed our approach to camp. We both made a great show about beginning our little camp tasks, but we did not last very long. The sun felt so good and it was so pleasant to lounge under a pine. One of the blessings of outdoor life was that a man could be like an Indian and do nothing. So from rest I passed to dreams and from dreams to sleep.

In the afternoon R. C. and I went out again to try for trout. The lake appeared to be getting thicker with that floating muck and we could not raise a fish. Then we tried the outlet again. Here the current was swift. I found a place between two willow banks where trout were breaking on the surface. It took a long cast for me, but about every tenth attempt I would get a fly over the right place and raise a fish. They were small, but that did not detract from my gratification. The light on the water was just right for me to see the trout rise, and that was a beautiful sight as well as a distinct advantage. I had caught four when a shout from R. C. called me quickly down stream. I found him standing in the middle of a swift chute with his rod bent double and a long line out.

"Got a whale!" he yelled. "See him—down there—in that white water. See him flash red! . . . Go down there and land him for me. Hurry! He's got all the line!"

I ran below to an open place in the willows. Here the stream was shallow and very swift. In the white water I caught a flashing gleam of red. Then I saw the shine of the leader. But I could not reach it without wading in. When I did this the trout lunged out. He looked crimson and silver. I could have put my fist in his mouth.

"Grab the leader! Yank him out!" yelled R. C. in desperation. "There! He's got all the line."

"But it'd be better to wade down," I yelled back.

He shouted that the water was too deep and for me to save his fish. This was an awful predicament for me. I knew the instant I grasped the leader that the big trout would break it or pull free. The same situation, with different kinds of fish, had presented itself many times on my numberless fishing jaunts with R. C. and they all crowded to my mind. Nevertheless I had no choice. Plunging in to my knees I frantically reached for the leader. The red trout made a surge. I missed him. R. C. yelled that something would break. That was no news to me. Then I essayed to lead the huge cutthroat ashore. He was heavy. But he was tired and that gave birth to hopes. Near the shore as I was about to lift him he woke up, swam round me twice, then ran between my legs.

When, a little later, R. C. came panting down stream I was sitting on the bank, all wet, with one knee skinned and I was holding his broken leader in my hands. Strange to say, he went into a rage! Blamed me for the loss of that big trout! Under such circumstances it was always best to maintain silence and I did so as long as I could. After his paroxysm had spent itself and he had become somewhat near a rational being once more he asked me:

"Was he big?"

"Oh—a whale of a trout!" I replied.

"Humph! Well, how big?"

Thereupon I enlarged upon the exceeding size and beauty of that trout. I made him out very much bigger than he actually looked to me and I minutely described his beauty and wonderful gaping mouth. R. C. groaned and that was my revenge.

We returned to camp early, and I took occasion to scrape acquaintance with the dogs. It was a strangely assorted pack—four Airedales, one bloodhound and seven other hounds of mixed breeds. There were also three pup hounds, white and yellow, very pretty dogs, and like all pups, noisy and mischievous. They made friends easily. This applied also to one of the Airedales, a dog recently presented to Teague by some estimable old lady who had called him Kaiser and made a pet of him. As might have been expected of a dog, even an Airedale, with that name, he was no good. But he was very affectionate, and exceedingly funny. When he was approached he had a trick of standing up, holding up his forepaws in an appealing sort of way, with his head twisted in the most absurd manner. This was when he was chained—otherwise he would have been climbing up on anyone who gave him the chance. He was the most jealous dog I ever saw. He could not be kept chained very long because he always freed himself. At meal time he would slip noiselessly behind some one and steal the first morsel he could snatch. Bill was always rapping Kaiser with pans or billets of firewood.

Next morning was clear and cold. We had breakfast, and then saddled up to ride to Big Fish Lake. For an hour we rode up and down ridges of heavy spruce, along a trail. We saw elk and deer sign. Elk tracks appeared almost as large as cow tracks. When we left the trail to climb into heavy timber we began to look for game. The forest was dark, green and brown, silent as a grave. No squirrels or birds or sign of life! We had a hard ride up and down steep slopes. A feature was the open swaths made by avalanches. The ice and snow had cut a path through the timber, and the young shoots of spruce were springing up. I imagined the roar made by that tremendous slide.

We found elk tracks everywhere and some fresh sign, where the grass had been turned recently, and also much old and fresh sign where the elk had skinned the saplings by rubbing their antlers to get rid of the velvet. Some of these rubs looked like blazes made by an axe. The Airedale Fox, a wonderful dog, routed out a she-coyote that evidently had a den somewhere, for she barked angrily at the dog and at us. Fox could not catch her. She led him round in a circle, and we could not see her in the thick brush. It was fine to hear the wild staccato note again.

We crossed many little parks, bright and green, blooming with wild asters and Indian paint brush and golden daisies. The patches of red and purple were exceedingly beautiful. Everywhere we rode we were knee deep in flowers. At length we came out of the heavy timber down upon Big Fish Lake. This lake was about half a mile across, deep blue-green in color, with rocky shores. Upon the opposite side were beaver mounds. We could see big trout swimming round, but they would not rise to a fly. R. C. went out in an old boat and paddled to the head of the lake and fished at the inlet. Here he caught a fine trout. I went around and up the little river that fed the lake. It curved swiftly through a meadow, and had deep, dark eddies under mossy, flowering banks. At other places the stream ran swiftly over clean gravel beds. It was musical and clear as crystal, and to the touch of hand, as cold as ice water. I waded in and began to cast. I saw several big trout, and at last coaxed one to take my fly. But I missed him. Then in a swift current a flash of red caught my eye and I saw a big trout lazily rise to my fly. Saw him take it! And I hooked him. He was not active, but heavy and plunging, and he bored in and out, and made short runs. I had not seen such beautiful red colors in any fish. He made a fine sight, but at last I landed him on the grass, a cutthroat of about one and three-quarter pounds, deep red and silver and green, and spotted all over. That was the extent of my luck.

We went back to the point, and thought we would wait a little while to see if the trout would begin to rise. But they did not. A storm began to mutter and boom along the battlements. Great gray clouds obscured the peaks, and at length the rain came. It was cold and cutting. We sought the shelter of spruces for a while, and waited. After an hour it cleared somewhat, and R. C. caught a fine one-pound cutthroat, all green and silver, with only two slashes of red along under the gills. Then another storm threatened. Before we got ready to leave for camp the rain began again to fall, and we looked for a wetting. It was raining hard when we rode into the woods and very cold. The spruces were dripping. But we soon got warm from hard riding up steep slopes. After an hour the rain ceased, the sun came out, and from the open places high up we could see a great green void of spruce, and beyond, boundless black ranges, running off to dim horizon. We flushed a big blue grouse with a brood of little ones, and at length another big one.

In one of the open parks the Airedale Fox showed signs of scenting game. There was a patch of ground where the grass was pressed down. Teague whispered and pointed. I saw the gray rump of an elk protruding from behind some spruces. I beckoned for R. C. and we both dismounted. Just then the elk rose and stalked out. It was a magnificent bull with crowning lofty antlers. The shoulders and neck appeared black. He raised his head, and turning, trotted away with ease and grace for such a huge beast. That was a wild and beautiful sight I had not seen before. We were entranced, and when he disappeared, we burst out with exclamations.

We rode on toward camp, and out upon a bench that bordered the lofty red wall of rock. From there we went down into heavy forest again, dim and gray, with its dank, penetrating odor, and oppressive stillness. The forest primeval! When we rode out of that into open slopes the afternoon was far advanced, and long shadows lay across the distant ranges. When we reached camp, supper and a fire to warm cold wet feet were exceedingly welcome. I was tired.

Later, R. C. and I rode up a mile or so above camp, and hitched our horses near Teague's old corral. Our intention was to hunt up along the side of the slope. Teague came along presently. We waited, hoping the big black clouds would break. But they did not. They rolled down with gray, swirling edges, like smoke, and a storm enveloped us. We sought shelter in a thick spruce. It rained and hailed. By and bye the air grew bitterly cold, and Teague suggested we give up, and ride back.

So we did. The mountains were dim and obscure through the gray gloom, and the black spear-tipped spruces looked ghostly against the background. The lightning was vivid, and the thunder rolled and crashed in magnificent bombardment across the heavens.

Next morning at six-thirty the sun was shining clear, and only a few clouds sailed in the blue. Wind was in the west and the weather promised fair. But clouds began to creep up behind the mountains, first hazy, then white, then dark. Nevertheless we decided to ride out, and cross the Flattop rim, and go around what they call the Chinese Wall. It rained as we climbed through the spruces above Little Trappers Lake. And as we got near the top it began to hail. Again the air grew cold. Once out on top I found a wide expanse, green and white, level in places, but with huge upheavals of ridge. There were flowers here at eleven thousand feet. The view to the rear was impressive—a wide up-and-down plain studded with out-cropping of rocks, and patches of snow. We were then on top of the Chinese Wall, and the view to the west was grand. At the moment hail was falling thick and white, and to stand above the streaked curtain, as it fell into the abyss was a strange new experience. Below, two thousand feet, lay the spruce forest, and it sloped and dropped into the White River Valley, which in turn rose, a long ragged dark-green slope, up to a bare jagged peak. Beyond this stretched range on range, dark under the lowering pall of clouds. On top we found fresh Rocky Mountain sheep tracks. A little later, going into a draw, we crossed a snow-bank, solid as ice. We worked down into this draw into the timber. It hailed, and rained some more, then cleared. The warm sun felt good. Once down in the parks we began to ride through a flower-garden. Every slope was beautiful in gold, and red, and blue and white. These parks were luxuriant with grass, and everywhere we found elk beds, where the great stags had been lying, to flee at our approach. But we did not see one. The bigness of this slope impressed me. We rode miles and miles, and every park was surrounded by heavy timber. At length we got into a burned district where the tall dead spruces stood sear and ghastly, and the ground was so thickly strewn with fallen trees that we had difficulty in threading a way through them. Patches of aspen grew on the hillside, still fresh and green despite this frosty morning. Here we found a sego lily, one of the most beautiful of flowers. Here also I saw pink Indian paint brush. At the foot of this long burned slope we came to the White River trail, and followed it up and around to camp.

Late in the evening, about sunset, I took my rifle and slipped off into the woods back of camp. I walked a short distance, then paused to listen to the silence of the forest. There was not a sound. It was a place of peace. By and bye I heard snapping of twigs, and presently heard R. C. and Teague approaching me. We penetrated half a mile into the spruce, pausing now and then to listen. At length R. C. heard something. We stopped. After a little I heard the ring of a horn on wood. It was thrilling. Then came the crack of a hoof on stone, then the clatter of a loosened rock. We crept on. But that elk or deer evaded us. We hunted around till dark without farther sign of any game.

R. C. and Teague and I rode out at seven-thirty and went down White River for three miles. In one patch of bare ground we saw tracks of five deer where they had come in for salt. Then we climbed high up a burned ridge, winding through patches of aspen. We climbed ridge after ridge, and at last got out of the burned district into reaches of heavy spruce. Coming to a park full of deer and elk tracks, we dismounted and left our horses. I went to the left, and into some beautiful woods, where I saw beds of deer or elk, and many tracks. Returning to the horses, I led them into a larger park, and climbed high into the open and watched. There I saw some little squirrels about three inches long, and some gray birds, very tame. I waited a long time before there was any sign of R. C. or Teague, and then it was the dog I saw first. I whistled, and they climbed up to me. We mounted and rode on for an hour, then climbed through a magnificent forest of huge trees, windfalls, and a ferny, mossy, soft ground. At length we came out at the head of a steep, bare slope, running down to a verdant park crossed by stretches of timber. On the way back to camp we ran across many elk beds and deer trails, and for a while a small band of elk evidently trotted ahead of us, but out of sight.

Next day we started for a few days' trip to Big Fish Lake. R. C. and I went along up around the mountain. I found our old trail, and was at a loss only a few times. We saw fresh elk sign, but no live game at all.

In the afternoon we fished. I went up the river half a mile, while R. C. fished the lake. Neither of us had any luck. Later we caught four trout, one of which was fair sized.

Toward sunset the trout began to rise all over the lake, but we could not get them to take a fly.

The following day we went up to Twin Lakes and found them to be beautiful little green gems surrounded by spruce. I saw some big trout in the large lake, but they were wary. We tried every way to get a strike. No use! In the little lake matters were worse. It was full of trout up to two pounds. They would run at the fly, only to refuse it. Exasperating work! We gave up and returned to Big Fish. After supper we went out to try again. The lake was smooth and quiet. All at once, as if by concert, the trout began to rise everywhere. In a little bay we began to get strikes. I could see the fish rise to the fly. The small ones were too swift and the large ones too slow, it seemed. We caught one, and then had bad luck. We snarled our lines, drifted wrong, broke leaders, snapped off flies, hooked too quick and too slow, and did everything that was clumsy. I lost two big fish because they followed the fly as I drew it toward me across the water to imitate a swimming fly. Of course this made a large slack line which I could not get up. Finally I caught one big fish, and altogether we got seven. All in that little bay, where the water was shallow! In other places we could not catch a fish. I had one vicious strike. The fish appeared to be feeding on a tiny black gnat, which we could not imitate. This was the most trying experience of all. We ought to have caught a basketful.

The next day, September first, we rode down along the outlet of Big Fish to White River and down that for miles to fish for grayling. The stream was large and swift and cold. It appeared full of ice water and rocks, but no fish. We met fishermen, an automobile, and a camp outfit. That was enough for me. Where an automobile can run, I do not belong. The fishing was poor. But the beautiful open valley, flowered in gold and purple, was recompense for a good deal of bad luck.

A grayling, or what they called a grayling, was not as beautiful a fish as my fancy had pictured. He resembled a sucker or mullet, had a small mouth, dark color, and was rather a sluggish-looking fish.

We rode back through a thunderstorm, and our yellow slickers afforded much comfort.

Next morning was bright, clear, cold. I saw the moon go down over a mountain rim rose-flushed with the sunrise.

R. C. and I, with Teague, started for the top of the big mountain on the west. I had a new horse, a roan, and he looked a thoroughbred. He appeared tired. But I thought he would be great. We took a trail through the woods, dark green-gray, cool and verdant, odorous and still. We began to climb. Occasionally we crossed parks, and little streams. Up near the long, bare slope the spruce trees grew large and far apart. They were beautiful, gray as if bearded with moss. Beyond this we got into the rocks and climbing became arduous. Long zigzags up the slope brought us to the top of a notch, where at the right lay a patch of snow. The top of the mountain was comparatively flat, but it had timbered ridges and bare plains and little lakes, with dark domes, rising beyond. We rode around to the right, climbing out of the timber to where the dwarf spruces and brush had a hard struggle for life. The great gulf below us was immense, dark, and wild, studded with lakes and parks, and shadowed by moving clouds.

Sheep tracks, old and fresh, afforded us thrills.

Away on the western rim, where we could look down upon a long rugged iron-gray ridge of mountain, our guide using the glass, found two big stags. We all had our fill of looking. I could see them plainly with naked eyes.

We decided to go back to where we could climb down on that side, halter the horses, leave all extra accoutrements, and stalk those stags, and take a picture of them.

I led the way, and descended under the rim. It was up and down over rough shale, and up steps of broken rocks, and down little cliffs. We crossed the ridge twice, many times having to lend a hand to each other.

At length I reached a point where I could see the stags lying down. The place was an open spot on a rocky promontory with a fringe of low spruces. The stags were magnificent in size, with antlers in the velvet. One had twelve points. They were lying in the sun to harden their horns, according to our guide.

I slipped back to the others, and we all decided to have a look. So we climbed up. All of us saw the stags, twitching ears and tails.

Then we crept back, and once more I took the lead to crawl round under the ledge so we could come up about even with them. Here I found the hardest going yet. I came to a wind-worn crack in the thin ledge, and from this I could just see the tips of the antlers. I beckoned the others. Laboriously they climbed. R. C. went through first. I went over next, and then came Teague.

R. C. and I started to crawl down to a big rock that was our objective point. We went cautiously, with bated breath and pounding hearts. When we got there I peeped over to see the stags still lying down. But they had heads intent and wary. Still I did not think they had scented us. R. C. took a peep, and turning excitedly he whispered:

"See only one. And he's standing!"

And I answered: "Let's get down around to the left where we can get a better chance." It was only a few feet down. We got there.

When he peeped over at this point he exclaimed: "They're gone!" It was a keen disappointment. "They winded us," I decided.

We looked and looked. But we could not see to our left because of the bulge of rock. We climbed back. Then I saw one of the stags loping leisurely off to the left. Teague was calling. He said they had walked off the promontory, looking up, and stopping occasionally.

Then we realized we must climb back along that broken ridge and then up to the summit of the mountain. So we started.

That climb back was proof of the effect of excitement on judgment. We had not calculated at all on the distance or ruggedness, and we had a job before us. We got along well under the western wall, and fairly well straight across through the long slope of timber, where we saw sheep tracks, and expected any moment to sight an old ram. But we did not find one, and when we got out of the timber upon the bare sliding slope we had to halt a hundred times. We could zigzag only a few steps. The altitude was twelve thousand feet, and oxygen seemed scarce. I nearly dropped. All the climbing appeared to come hardest on the middle of my right foot, and it could scarcely have burned hotter if it had been in fire. Despite the strenuous toil there were not many moments that I was not aware of the vastness of the gulf below, or the peaceful lakes, brown as amber, or the golden parks. And nearer at hand I found magenta-colored Indian paint brush, very exquisite and rare.

Coming out on a ledge I spied a little, dark animal with a long tail. He was running along the opposite promontory about three hundred yards distant. When he stopped I took a shot at him and missed by apparently a scant half foot.

After catching our breath we climbed more and more, and still more, at last to drop on the rim, hot, wet and utterly spent.

The air was keen, cold, and invigorating. We were soon rested, and finding our horses we proceeded along the rim westward. Upon rounding an outcropping of rock we flushed a flock of ptarmigan—soft gray, rock-colored birds about the size of pheasants, and when they flew they showed beautiful white bands on their wings. These are the rare birds that have feathered feet and turn white in winter. They did not fly far, and several were so tame they did not fly at all. We got our little .22 revolvers and began to shoot at the nearest bird. He was some thirty feet distant. But we could not hit him, and at last Fox, getting disgusted, tried to catch the bird and made him fly. I felt relieved, for as we were getting closer and closer with every shot, it seemed possible that if the ptarmigan sat there long enough we might eventually have hit him. The mystery was why we shot so poorly. But this was explained by R. C., who discovered we had been shooting the wrong shells.

It was a long hard ride down the rough winding trail. But riding down was a vastly different thing from going up.

On September third we were up at five-thirty. It was clear and cold and the red of sunrise tinged the peaks. The snow banks looked pink. All the early morning scene was green, fresh, cool, with that mountain rareness of atmosphere.

We packed to break camp, and after breakfast it took hours to get our outfit in shape to start—a long string, resembling a caravan. I knew that events would occur that day. First we lost one of the dogs. Vern went back after him. The dogs were mostly chained in pairs, to prevent their running off. Samson, the giant hound, was chained to a little dog, and the others were paired not according to size by any means. The poor dogs were disgusted with the arrangement. It developed presently that Cain, the bloodhound, a strange and wild hound much like Don of my old lion-hunting days, slipped us, and was not missed for hours. Teague decided to send back for him later.

Next in order of events, as we rode up the winding trail through the spruce forest, we met Teague's cow and calf, which he had kept all summer in camp. For some reason neither could be left. Teague told us to ride on, and an hour later when we halted to rest on the Flattop Mountain he came along with the rest of the train, and in the fore was the cow alone. It was evident that she was distressed and angry, for it took two men to keep her in the trail. And another thing plain to me was the fact that she was going to demoralize the pack horses. We were not across the wide range of this flat mountain when one of the pack animals, a lean and lanky sorrel, appeared suddenly to go mad, and began to buck off a pack. He succeeded. This inspired a black horse, very appropriately christened Nigger, to try his luck, and he shifted his pack in short order. It took patience, time, and effort to repack. The cow was a disorganizer. She took up as wide a trail as a road. And the pack animals, some with dignity and others with disgust, tried to avoid her vicinity. Going down the steep forest trail on the other side the real trouble began. The pack train split, ran and bolted, crashing through the trees, plunging down steep places, and jumping logs. It was a wild sort of chase. But luckily the packs remained intact until we were once more on open, flat ground. All went well for a while, except for an accident for which I was to blame. I spurred my horse, and he plunged suddenly past R. C.'s mount, colliding with him, tearing off my stirrup, and spraining R. C.'s ankle. This was almost a serious accident, as R. C. has an old baseball ankle that required favoring.

Next in order was the sorrel. As I saw it, he heedlessly went too near the cow, which we now called Bossy, and she acted somewhat like a Spanish Bull, to the effect that the sorrel was scared and angered at once. He began to run and plunge and buck right into the other pack animals, dropping articles from his pack as he dashed along. He stampeded the train, and gave the saddle horses a scare. When order was restored and the whole outfit gathered together again a full hour had been lost. By this time all the horses were tired, and that facilitated progress, because there were no more serious breaks.

Down in the valley it was hot, and the ride grew long and wearisome. Nevertheless, the scenery was beautiful. The valley was green and level, and a meandering stream formed many little lakes. On one side was a steep hill of sage and aspens, and on the other a black, spear-pointed spruce forest, rising sheer to a bold, blunt peak patched with snow-banks, and bronze and gray in the clear light. Huge white clouds sailed aloft, making dark moving shadows along the great slopes.

We reached our turning-off place about five o'clock, and again entered the fragrant, quiet forest—a welcome change. We climbed and climbed, at length coming into an open park of slopes and green borders of forest, with a lake in the center. We pitched camp on the skirt of the western slope, under the spruces, and worked hard to get the tents up and boughs cut for beds. Darkness caught us with our hands still full, and we ate supper in the light of a camp-fire, with the black, deep forest behind, and the pale afterglow across the lake.

I had a bad night, being too tired to sleep well. Many times I saw the moon shadows of spruce branches trembling on the tent walls, and the flickering shadows of the dying camp-fire. I heard the melodious tinkle of the bells on the hobbled horses. Bossy bawled often—a discordant break in the serenity of the night. Occasionally the hounds bayed her.

Toward morning I slept some, and awakened with what seemed a broken back. All, except R. C., were slow in crawling out. The sun rose hot. This lower altitude was appreciated by all. After breakfast we set to work to put the camp in order.

That afternoon we rode off to look over the ground. We crossed the park and worked up a timbered ridge remarkable for mossy, bare ground, and higher up for its almost total absence of grass or flowers. On the other side of this we had a fine view of Mt. Dome, a high peak across a valley. Then we worked down into the valley, which was full of parks and ponds and running streams. We found some fresh sign of deer, and a good deal of old elk and deer sign. But we saw no game of any kind. It was a tedious ride back through thick forest, where I observed many trees that had been barked by porcupines. Some patches were four feet from the ground, indicating that the porcupine had sat on the snow when he gnawed those particular places.

After sunset R. C. and I went off down a trail into the woods, and sitting down under a huge spruce we listened. The forest was solemn and still. Far down somewhere roared a stream, and that was all the sound we heard. The gray shadows darkened and gloom penetrated the aisles of the forest, until all the sheltered places were black as pitch. The spruces looked spectral—and speaking. The silence of the woods was deep, profound, and primeval. It all worked on my imagination until I began to hear faint sounds, and finally grand orchestral crashings of melody.

On our return the strange creeping chill, that must be a descendant of the old elemental fear, caught me at all obscure curves in the trail.

Next day we started off early, and climbed through the woods and into the parks under the Dome. We scared a deer that had evidently been drinking. His fresh tracks led before us, but we could not catch a glimpse of him.

We climbed out of the parks, up onto the rocky ridges where the spruce grew scarce, and then farther to the jumble of stones that had weathered from the great peaks above, and beyond that up the slope where all the vegetation was dwarfed, deformed, and weird, strange manifestation of its struggle for life. Here the air grew keener and cooler, and the light seemed to expand. We rode on to the steep slope that led up to the gap we were to cross between the Dome and its companion.

I saw a red fox running up the slope, and dismounting I took a quick shot at three hundred yards, and scored a hit. It turned out to be a cross fox, and had very pretty fur.

When we reached the level of the deep gap the wind struck us hard and cold. On that side opened an abyss, gray and shelving as it led down to green timber, and then on to the yellow parks and black ridges that gleamed under the opposite range.

We had to work round a wide amphitheater, and up a steep corner to the top. This turned out to be level and smooth for a long way, with a short, velvety yellow grass, like moss, spotted with flowers. Here at thirteen thousand feet, the wind hit us with exceeding force, and soon had us with freezing hands and faces. All about us were bold black and gray peaks, with patches of snow, and above them clouds of white and drab, showing blue sky between. It developed that this grassy summit ascended in a long gradual sweep, from the apex of which stretched a grand expanse, like a plain of gold, down and down, endlessly almost, and then up and up to end under a gray butte, highest of the points around. The ride across here seemed to have no limit, but it was beautiful, though severe on endurance. I saw another fox, and dismounting, fired five shots as he ran, dusting him with three bullets. We rode out to the edge of the mountain and looked off. It was fearful, yet sublime. The world lay beneath us. In many places we rode along the rim, and at last circled the great butte, and worked up behind it on a swell of slope. Here the range ran west and the drop was not sheer, but gradual with fine benches for sheep. We found many tracks and fresh sign, but did not see one sheep. Meanwhile the hard wind had ceased, and the sun had come out, making the ride comfortable, as far as weather was concerned. We had gotten a long way from camp, and finding no trail to descend in that direction we turned to retrace our steps. That was about one o'clock, and we rode and rode and rode until I was so tired that I could not appreciate the scenes as I had on the way up. It took six hours to get back to camp!

Next morning we took the hounds and rode off for bear. Eight of the hounds were chained in braces, one big and one little dog together, and they certainly had a hard time of it. Sampson, the giant gray and brown hound, and Jim, the old black leader, were free to run to and fro across the way. We rode down a few miles, and into the forest. There were two long, black ridges, and here we were to hunt for bear. It was the hardest kind of work, turning and twisting between the trees, dodging snags, and brushing aside branches, and guiding a horse among fallen logs. The forest was thick, and the ground was a rich brown and black muck, soft to the horses' feet. Many times the hounds got caught on snags, and had to be released. Once Sampson picked up a scent of some kind, and went off baying. Old Jim ran across that trail and returned, thus making it clear that there was no bear trail. We penetrated deep between the two ridges, and came to a little lake, about thirty feet wide, surrounded by rushes and grass. Here we rested the horses, and incidentally, ourselves. Fox chased a duck, and it flew into the woods and hid under a log. Fox trailed it, and Teague shot it just as he might have a rabbit. We got two more ducks, fine big mallards, the same way. It

was amazing to me, and R. C. remarked that never had he seen such strange and foolish ducks.

This forest had hundreds of trees barked by porcupines, and some clear to the top. But we met only one of the animals, and he left several quills in the nose of one of the pups. I was of the opinion that these porcupines destroy many fine trees, as I saw a number barked all around.

We did not see any bear sign. On the way back to camp we rode out of the forest and down a wide valley, the opposite side of which was open slope with patches of alder. Even at a distance I could discern the color of these open glades and grassy benches. They had a tinge of purple, like purple sage. When I got to them I found a profusion of asters of the most exquisite shades of lavender, pink and purple. That slope was long, and all the way up we rode through these beautiful wild flowers. I shall never forget that sight, nor the many asters that shone like stars out of the green. The pink ones were new to me, and actually did not seem real. I noticed my horse occasionally nipped a bunch and ate them, which seemed to me almost as heartless as to tread them under foot.

When we got up the slope and into the woods again we met a storm, and traveled for an hour in the rain, and under the dripping spruces, feeling the cold wet sting of swaying branches as we rode by. Then the sun came out bright and the forest glittered, all gold and green. The smell of the woods after a rain is indescribable. It combines a rare tang of pine, spruce, earth and air, all refreshed.

The day after, we left at eight o'clock, and rode down to the main trail, and up that for five miles where we cut off to the left and climbed into the timber. The woods were fresh and dewy, dark and cool, and for a long time we climbed bench after bench where the grass and ferns and moss made a thick, deep cover. Farther up we got into fallen timber and made slow progress. At timber line we tied the horses and climbed up to the pass between two great mountain ramparts. Sheep tracks were in evidence, but not very fresh. Teague and I climbed on top and R. C., with Vern, went below just along the timber line. The climb on foot took all my strength, and many times I had to halt for breath. The air was cold. We stole along the rim and peered over. R. C. and Vern looked like very little men far below, and the dogs resembled mice.

Teague climbed higher, and left me on a promontory, watching all around.

The cloud pageant was magnificent, with huge billowy white masses across the valley, and to the west great black thunderheads rolling up. The wind began to blow hard, carrying drops of rain that stung, and the air was nipping cold. I felt aloof from all the crowded world, alone on the windy heights, with clouds and storm all around me.

When the storm threatened I went back to the horses. It broke, but was not severe after all. At length R. C. and the men returned and we mounted to ride back to camp. The storm blew away, leaving the sky clear and blue, and the sun shone warm. We had an hour of winding in and out among windfalls of timber, and jumping logs, and breaking through brush. Then the way sloped down to a beautiful forest, shady and green, full of mossy dells, almost overgrown with ferns and low spreading ground pine or spruce. The aisles of the forest were long and shaded by the stately spruces. Water ran through every ravine, sometimes a brawling brook, sometimes a rivulet hidden under overhanging mossy banks. We scared up two lonely grouse, at long intervals. At length we got into fallen timber, and from that worked into a jumble of rocks, where the going was rough and dangerous.

The afternoon waned as we rode on and on, up and down, in and out, around, and at times the horses stood almost on their heads, sliding down steep places where the earth was soft and black, and gave forth a dank odor. We passed ponds and swamps, and little lakes. We saw where beavers had gnawed down aspens, and we just escaped miring our horses in marshes, where the grass grew, rich and golden, hiding the treacherous mire. The sun set, and still we did not seem to get anywhere. I was afraid darkness would overtake us, and we would get lost in the woods. Presently we struck an old elk trail, and following that for a while, came to a point where R. C. and I recognized a tree and a glade where we had been before—and not far from camp—a welcome discovery.

Next day we broke camp and started across country for new territory near Whitley's Peak.

We rode east up the mountain. After several miles along an old logging road we reached the timber, and eventually the top of the ridge. We went down, crossing parks and swales. There were cattle pastures, and eaten over and trodden so much they had no beauty left. Teague wanted to camp at a salt lick, but I did not care for the place.

We went on. The dogs crossed a bear trail, and burst out in a clamor. We had a hard time holding them.

The guide and I had a hot argument. I did not want to stay there and chase a bear in a cow pasture. . . . So we went on, down into ranch country, and this disgusted me further. We crossed a ranch, and rode several miles on a highway, then turned abruptly, and climbed a rough, rocky ridge, covered with brush and aspen. We crossed it, and went down for several miles, and had to camp in an aspen grove, on the slope of a ravine. It was an uninviting place to stay, but as there was no other we had to make the best of it. The afternoon had waned. I took a gun and went off down the ravine, until I came to a deep gorge. Here I heard the sound of a brawling brook. I sat down for an hour, but saw no game.

That night I had a wretched bed, one that I could hardly stay in, and I passed miserable hours. I got up sore, cramped, sleepy and irritable. We had to wait three hours for the horses to be caught and packed. I had predicted straying horses. At last we were off, and rode along the steep slope of a canyon for several miles, and then struck a stream of amber-colored water. As we climbed along this we came into deep spruce forest, where it was pleasure to ride. I saw many dells and nooks, cool and shady, full of mossy rocks and great trees. But flowers were scarce. We were sorry to pass the head-springs of that stream and to go on over the divide and down into the wooded, but dry and stony country. We rode until late, and came at last to a park where sheep had been run. I refused to camp here, and Teague, in high dudgeon, rode on. As it turned out I was both wise and lucky, for we rode into a park with many branches, where there was good water and fair grass and a pretty grove of white pines in which to pitch our tents. I enjoyed this camp, and had a fine rest at night.

The morning broke dark and lowering. We hustled to get started before a storm broke. It began to rain as we mounted our horses, and soon we were in the midst of a cold rain. It blew hard. We put on our slickers. After a short ride down through the forest we entered Buffalo Park. This was a large park, and we lost time trying to find a forester's trail leading out of it. At last we found one, but it soon petered out, and we were lost in thick timber, in a driving rain, with the cold and wind increasing. But we kept on.

This forest was deep and dark, with tremendous windfalls, and great canyons around which we had to travel. It took us hours to ride out of it. When we began to descend once more we struck an old lumber road. More luck—the storm ceased, and presently we were out on an aspen slope with a great valley beneath, and high, black peaks beyond.

Below the aspens were long swelling slopes of sage and grass, gray and golden and green. A ranch lay in the valley, and we crossed it to climb up a winding ravine, once more to the aspens where we camped in the rancher's pasture. It was a cold, wet camp, but we managed to be fairly comfortable.

The sunset was gorgeous. The mass of clouds broke and rolled. There was exquisite golden light on the peaks, and many rose- and violet-hued banks of cloud.

Morning found us shrouded in fog. We were late starting. About nine the curtain of gray began to lift and break. We climbed pastures and aspen thickets, high up to the spruce, where the grass grew luxuriant, and the red wall of rock overhung the long slopes. The view west was magnificent—a long, bulging range of mountains, vast stretches of green aspen slopes, winding parks of all shapes, gray and gold and green, and jutting peaks, and here and there patches of autumn blaze in grass and thicket.

We spent the afternoon pitching camp on an aspen knoll, with water, grass, and wood near at hand, and the splendid view of mountains and valleys below.

We spent many full days under the shadow of Whitley's Peak. After the middle of September the aspens colored and blazed to the touch of frost, and the mountain slopes were exceedingly beautiful. Against a background of gray sage the gold and red and purple aspen groves showed too much like exquisite paintings to seem real. In the mornings the frost glistened thick and white on the grass; and after the gorgeous sunsets of gold over the violet-hazed ranges the air grew stingingly cold.

Bear-chasing with a pack of hounds has been severely criticised by many writers and I was among them. I believed it a cowardly business, and that was why, if I chased bears with dogs, I wanted to chase the kind that could not be treed. But like many another I did not know what I was writing about. I did not shoot a bear out of a tree and I would not do so, except in a case of hunger. All the same, leaving the tree out of consideration, bear-chasing with hounds is a tremendously exciting and hazardous game. But my ideas about sport are changing. Hunting, in the sportsman's sense, is a cruel and degenerate business.

The more I hunt the more I become convinced of something wrong about the game. I am a different man when I get a gun in my hands. All is exciting, hot-pressed, red. Hunting is magnificent up to the moment the shot is fired. After that it is another matter. It is useless for sportsmen to tell me that they, in particular, hunt right, conserve the game, do not go beyond the limit, and all that sort of thing. I do not believe them and I never met the guide who did. A rifle is made for killing. When a man goes out with one he means to kill. He may keep within the law, but that is not the question. It is a question of spirit, and men who love to hunt are yielding to and always developing the old primitive instinct to kill. The meaning of the spirit of life is not clear to them. An argument may be advanced that, according to the laws of self-preservation and the survival of the fittest, if a man stops all strife, all fight, then he will retrograde. And that is to say if a man does not go to the wilds now and then, and work hard and live some semblance of the life of his progenitors, he will weaken. It seems that he will, but I am not prepared now to say whether or not that would be well. The Germans believe they are the race fittest to survive over all others—and that has made me a little sick of this Darwin business.

To return, however, to the fact that to ride after hounds on a wild chase is a dangerous and wonderfully exhilarating experience, I will relate a couple of instances, and I will leave it to my readers to judge whether or not it is a cowardly sport.

One afternoon a rancher visited our camp and informed us that he had surprised a big black bear eating the carcass of a dead cow.

"Good! We'll have a bear to-morrow night," declared Teague, in delight. "We'll get him even if the trail is a day old. But he'll come back to-night."

Early the next morning the young rancher and three other boys rode into camp, saying they would like to go with us to see the fun. We were glad to have them, and we rode off through the frosted sage that crackled like brittle glass under the hoofs of the horses. Our guide led toward a branch of a park, and when we got within perhaps a quarter of a mile Teague suggested that R. C. and I go ahead on the chance of surprising the bear. It was owing to this suggestion that my brother and I were well ahead of the others. But we did not see any bear near the carcass of the cow. Old Jim and Sampson were close behind us, and when Jim came within forty yards of that carcass he put his nose up with a deep and ringing bay, and he shot by us like a streak. He never went near the dead cow! Sampson bayed like thunder and raced after Jim.

"They're off!" I yelled to R. C. "It's a hot scent! Come on!"

We spurred our horses and they broke across the open park to the edge of the woods. Jim and Sampson were running straight with noses high. I heard a string of yelps and bellows from our rear.

"Look back!" shouted R. C.

Teague and the cowboys were unleashing the rest of the pack. It surely was great to see them stretch out, yelping wildly. Like the wind they passed us. Jim and Sampson headed into the woods with deep bays. I was riding Teague's best horse for this sort of work and he understood the game and plainly enjoyed it. R. C.'s horse ran as fast in the woods as he did in the open. This frightened me, and I yelled to R. C. to be careful. I yelled to deaf ears. That is the first great risk—a rider is not going to be careful! We were right on top of Jim and Sampson with the pack clamoring mad music just behind. The forest rang. Both horses hurdled logs, sometimes two at once. My old lion chases with Buffalo Jones had made me skillful in dodging branches and snags, and sliding knees back to avoid knocking them against trees For a mile the forest was comparatively open, and here we had a grand and ringing run. I received two hard knocks, was unseated once, but held on, and I got a stinging crack in the face from a branch. R. C. added several more black-and-blue spots to his already spotted anatomy, and he missed, just by an inch, a solid snag that would have broken him in two. The pack stretched out in wild staccato chorus, the little Airedales literally screeching. Jim got out of our sight and then Sampson. Still it was ever more thrilling to follow by sound rather than sight. They led up a thick, steep slope. Here we got into trouble in the windfalls of timber and the pack drew away from us, up over the mountain. We were half way up when we heard them jump the bear. The forest seemed full of strife and bays and yelps. We heard the dogs go down again to our right, and as we turned we saw Teague and the others strung out along the edge of the park. They got far ahead of us. When we reached the bottom of the slope they were out of sight, but we could hear them yell. The hounds were working around on another slope, from which craggy rocks loomed above the timber. R. C.'s horse lunged across the park and appeared to be running off from mine. I was a little to the right, and when my horse got under way, full speed, we had the bad luck to plunge suddenly into soft ground. He went to his knees, and I sailed out of the saddle fully twenty feet, to alight all spread out and to slide like a plow. I did not seem to be hurt. When I got up my horse was coming and he appeared to be patient with me, but he was in a hurry. Before we got across the wet place R. C. was out of sight. I decided that instead of worrying about him I had better think about myself. Once on hard ground my horse fairly charged into the woods and we broke brush and branches as if they had been punk. It was again open forest, then a rocky slope, and then a flat ridge with aisles between the trees. Here I heard the melodious notes of Teague's hunting horn, and following that, the full chorus of the hounds. They had treed the bear. Coming into still more open forest, with rocks here and there, I caught sight of R. C. far ahead, and soon I had glimpses of the other horses, and lastly, while riding full tilt, I spied a big, black, glistening bear high up in a pine a hundred yards or more distant.

Slowing down I rode up to the circle of frenzied dogs and excited men. The boys were all jabbering at once. Teague was beaming. R. C. sat his horse, and it struck me that he looked sorry for the bear.

"Fifteen minutes!" ejaculated Teague, with a proud glance at Old Jim standing with forepaws up on the pine.

Indeed it had been a short and ringing chase.

All the time while I fooled around trying to photograph the treed bear, R. C. sat there on his horse, looking upward.

"Well, gentlemen, better kill him," said Teague, cheerfully. "If he gets rested he'll come down."

It was then I suggested to R. C. that he do the shooting.

"Not much!" he exclaimed.

The bear looked really pretty perched up there. He was as round as a barrel and black as jet and his fur shone in the gleams of sunlight. His tongue hung out, and his plump sides heaved, showing what a quick, hard run he had made before being driven to the tree. What struck me most forcibly about him was the expression in his eyes as he looked down at those devils of hounds. He was scared. He realized his peril. It was utterly impossible for me to see Teague's point of view.

"Go ahead—and plug him," I replied to my brother. "Get it over."

"You do it," he said.

"No, I won't."

"Why not—I'd like to know?"

"Maybe we won't have so good a chance again—and I want you to get your bear," I replied.

"Why it's like—murder," he protested.

"Oh, not so bad as that," I returned, weakly. "We need the meat.

We've not had any game meat, you know, except ducks and grouse."

"You won't do it?" he added, grimly.

"No, I refuse."

Meanwhile the young ranchers gazed at us with wide eyes and the expression on Teague's honest, ruddy face would have been funny under other circumstances.

"That bear will come down an' mebbe kill one of my dogs," he protested.

"Well, he can come for all I care," I replied, positively, and I turned away.

I heard R. C. curse low under his breath. Then followed the spang of his .35 Remington. I wheeled in time to see the bear straining upward in terrible convulsion, his head pointed high, with blood spurting from his nose. Slowly he swayed and fell with a heavy crash.

The next bear chase we had was entirely different medicine.

Off in the basin under the White Slides, back of our camp, the hounds struck a fresh track and in an instant were out of sight. With the cowboy Vern setting the pace we plunged after them. It was rough country. Bogs, brooks, swales, rocky little parks, stretches of timber full of windfalls, groves of aspens so thick we could scarcely squeeze through—all these obstacles soon allowed the hounds to get far away. We came out into a large park, right under the mountain slope, and here we sat our horses listening to the chase. That trail led around the basin and back near to us, up the thick green slope, where high up near a ledge we heard the pack jump this bear. It sounded to us as if he had been roused out of a sleep.

"I'll bet it's one of the big grizzlies we've heard about," said Teague.

That was something to my taste. I have seen a few grizzlies. Riding to higher ground I kept close watch on the few open patches up on the slope. The chase led toward us for a while. Suddenly I saw a big bear with a frosted coat go lumbering across one of these openings.

"Silvertip! Silvertip!" I yelled at the top of my lungs. "I saw him!"

My call thrilled everybody. Vern spurred his horse and took to the right. Teague advised that we climb the slope. So we made for the timber. Once there we had to get off and climb on foot. It was steep, rough, very hard work. I had on chaps and spurs. Soon I was hot, laboring, and my heart began to hurt. We all had to rest. The baying of the hounds inspirited us now and then, but presently we lost it. Teague said they had gone over the ridge and as soon as we got up to the top we would hear them again. We struck an elk trail with fresh elk tracks in it. Teague said they were just ahead of us. I never climbed so hard and fast in my life. We were all tuckered out when we reached the top of the ridge. Then to our great disappointment we did not hear the hounds. Mounting we rode along the crest of this wooded ridge toward the western end, which was considerably higher. Once on a bare patch of ground we saw where the grizzly had passed. The big, round tracks, toeing in a little, made a chill go over me. No doubt of its being a silvertip!

We climbed and rode to the high point, and coming out upon the summit of the mountain we all heard the deep, hoarse baying of the pack. They were in the canyon down a bare grassy slope and over a wooded bench at our feet. Teague yelled as he spurred down. R. C. rode hard in his tracks.

But my horse was new to this bear chasing. He was mettlesome, and he did not want to do what I wanted. When I jabbed the spurs into his flanks he nearly bucked me off. I was looking for a soft place to light when he quit. Long before I got down that open slope Teague and R. C. had disappeared. I had to follow their tracks. This I did at a gallop, but now and then lost the tracks, and had to haul in to find them. If I could have heard the hounds from there I would have gone on anyway. But once down in the jack-pines I could hear neither yell or bay. The pines were small, close together, and tough. I hurt my hands, scratched my face, barked my knees. The horse had a habit of suddenly deciding to go the way he liked instead of the way I guided him, and when he plunged between saplings too close together to permit us both

to go through, it was exceedingly hard on me. I was worked into a frenzy. Suppose R. C. should come face to face with that old grizzly and fail to kill him! That was the reason for my desperate hurry. I got a crack on the head that nearly blinded me. My horse grew hot and began to run in every little open space. He could scarcely be held in. And I, with the blood hot in me too, did not hold him hard enough.

It seemed miles across that wooded bench. But at last I reached another slope. Coming out upon a canyon rim I heard R. C. and Teague yelling, and I heard the hounds fighting the grizzly. He was growling and threshing about far below. I had missed the tracks made by Teague and my brother, and it was necessary to find them. That slope looked impassable. I rode back along the rim, then forward. Finally I found where the ground was plowed deep and here I headed my horse. He had been used to smooth roads and he could not take these jumps. I went forward on his neck. But I hung on and spurred him hard. The mad spirit of that chase had gotten into him too. All the time I could hear the fierce baying and yelping of the hounds, and occasionally I heard a savage bawl from the bear. I literally plunged, slid, broke a way down that mountain slope, riding all the time, before I discovered the footprints of Teague and R. C. They had walked, leading their horses. By this time I was so mad I would not get off. I rode all the way down that steep slope of dense saplings, loose rock slides and earth, and jumble of splintered cliff. That he did not break my neck and his own spoke the truth about that roan horse. Despite his inexperience he was great. We fell over one bank, but a thicket of aspens saved us from rolling. The avalanches slid from under us until I imagined that the grizzly would be scared. Once as I stopped to listen I heard bear and pack farther down the canyon—heard them above the roar of a rushing stream. They went on and I lost the sounds of fight. But R. C.'s clear thrilling call floated up to me. Probably he was worried about me.

Then before I realized it I was at the foot of the slope, in a narrow canyon bed, full of rocks and trees, with the din of roaring water in my ears. I could hear nothing else. Tracks were everywhere, and when I came to the first open place I was thrilled. The grizzly had plunged off a sandy bar into the water, and there he had fought the hounds. Signs of that battle were easy to read. I saw where his huge tracks, still wet, led up the opposite sandy bank.

Then, down stream, I did my most reckless riding. On level ground the horse was splendid. Once he leaped clear across the brook. Every plunge, every turn I expected to bring me upon my brother and Teague and that fighting pack. More than once I thought I heard the sprang of the .35 and this made me urge the roan faster and faster.

The canyon narrowed, the stream-bed deepened. I had to slow down to get through the trees and rocks. And suddenly I was overjoyed to ride pell-mell upon R. C. and Teague with half the panting hounds. The canyon had grown too rough for the horses to go farther and it would have been useless for us to try on foot. As I dismounted, so sore and bruised I could hardly stand, old Jim came limping in to fall into the brook where he lapped and lapped thirstily. Teague threw up his hands. Old Jim's return meant an ended chase. The grizzly had eluded the hounds in that jumble of rocks below.

"Say, did you meet the bear?" queried Teague, eyeing me in astonishment and mirth.

Bloody, dirty, ragged and wringing wet with sweat I must have been a sight. R. C. however, did not look so very immaculate, and when I saw he also was lame and scratched and black I felt better.

ENOS MILLS.

1920

One of the few reminders today of Enos Mills's tremendous contributions to conservation in Colorado is a small log cabin south of Estes Park on the Peak-to-Peak Highway. The cabin—as well as the comparative obscurity of Mills's name among the ranks of famous naturalists—belies the great popularity of his writing in the early years of this century. In his day Mills was an ardent advocate of conservation in general, and the concept of a national park system in particular. More significantly, he was known to not just a few as the "father of Rocky Mountain National Park."

The title was well-deserved, for no other person before or since could claim to have known the region surrounding Longs Peak as well as Mills had. Setting out alone at the age of fourteen from his native Kansas in 1884, he went first to Colorado and supported himself by working at hotels and ranches in the Estes Park area. Survey work next took him throughout the West from Montana to the Pacific, but in the 1890s he returned to the area that had first captured his imagination, the Colorado Front Range. As innkeeper and guide, Mills quickly developed an ability for interpreting natural phenomena for the uninitiated—a talent that later led to a successful writing career.

Mills's reputation as a conservationist might have advanced farther had not a bizarre accident taken his life just as he began to contribute to the national debate over parks policy. While visiting New York City in 1922 he was fatally injured in a subway accident—an ironic end to a life that had seen far greater perils in the wild. The following selection, "Snowblinded on the Summit," describes one such life-and-death experience, but the breathless tension of the adventure is relieved by his expansive knowledge and love of the natural world.

SNOW-BLINDED
ON THE SUMMIT

As I CLIMBED UP OUT OF
the dwarfed woods at timberline in the Rocky Mountains, and started
across the treeless white summit, the terrific sun glare on the snow
warned me of the danger of snow-blindness. I had lost my snow glasses.
But the wild attractions of the heights caused me to forget the care of
my eyes and I lingered to look down into cañons and to examine mag-
ificent snow cornices. A number of mountain sheep also interested me.
Then for half an hour I circled a confiding flock of ptarmigan and took
picture after picture.

Through the clear air the sunlight poured with burning intensity.
I was 12,000 feet above the sea. Around me there was not a dark crag
nor even a tree to absorb the excess of light. A wilderness of high, rugged
peaks stood about—splendid sunlit mountains of snow. To east and west
they faced winter's noonday sun with great shadow mantles flowing
from their shoulders.

As I started to hurry on across the pass I began to experience the
scorching pains that go with seared, sunburnt eyes—snow-blindness.
Unfortunately, I had failed to take even the precaution of blackening
my face, which would have dulled the glare. At the summit my eyes
became so painful that I could endure the light only a few seconds at
a time. Occasionally I sat down and closed them for a minute or two.
Finally, while doing this, the lids adhered to the balls and the eyes swelled
so that I could not open them.

Blind on the summit of the Continental Divide! I made a grab for
my useful staff which I had left standing beside me in the snow. In the
fraction of a second that elapsed between thinking of the staff and find-

Reprinted by permission of Enda Mills Kiley, from *Adventures of a Nature Guide* (1920).
Copyright renewed 1978.

ing it my brain woke up to the seriousness of the situation. To the nearest trees it was more than a mile, and the nearest house was many miles away across ridges of rough mountains. I had matches and a hatchet, but no provisions. Still, while well aware of my peril, I was only moderately excited, feeling no terror. Less startling incidents have shocked me more, narrow escapes from street automobiles have terrified me.

It had been a wondrous morning. The day cleared after a heavy fall of fluffy snow. I had snowshoed up the slope through a ragged, snow-carpeted spruce forest, whose shadows wrought splendid black-and-white effects upon the shining floor. There were thousands of towering, slender spruces, each brilliantly laden with snow flowers, standing soft, white, and motionless in the sunlight. While I was looking at one of these artistically decorated trees, a mass of snow dropped upon me from its top, throwing me headlong and causing me to lose my precious eye-protecting snow glasses. But now I was blind.

With staff in hand, I stood for a minute or two planning the best manner to get along without eyes. My faculties were intensely awake. Serious situations in the wilds had more than once before this stimulated them to do their best. Temporary blindness is a good stimulus for the imagination and the memory—in fact, is good educational training for all the senses. However perilous my predicament during a mountain trip, the possibility of a fatal ending never even occurred to me. Looking back now, I cannot but wonder at my matter-of-fact attitude concerning the perils in which that snow-blindness placed me.

I had planned to cross the pass and descend into a trail at timberline. The appearance of the slope down which I was to travel was distinctly in my mind from my impressions just before darkness settled over me.

Off I slowly started. I guided myself with information from feet and staff, feeling my way with the staff so as not to step off a cliff or walk overboard into a cañon. In imagination I pictured myself following the shadow of a staff-bearing and slouch-hatted form. Did mountain sheep, curious and slightly suspicious, linger on crags to watch my slow and hesitating advance? Across the snow did the shadow of a soaring eagle coast and circle?

I must have wandered far from the direct course to timberline. Again and again I swung my staff to right and left hoping to strike a tree. I had travelled more than twice as long as it should have taken to reach timberline before I stood face to face with a low-growing tree that bristled up through the deep snow. But had I come out at the point for which I aimed—at the trail? This was the vital question.

The deep snow buried all trail blazes. Making my way from tree to tree I thrust an arm deep into the snow and felt of the bark, searching for a trail blaze. At last I found a blaze and going on a few steps I dug down again in the snow and examined a tree which I felt should mark the trail. This, too, was blazed.

Feeling certain that I was on the trail I went down the mountain through the forest for some minutes without searching for another blaze. When I did examine a number of trees not another blaze could I find. The topography since entering the forest and the size and character of the trees were such that I felt I was on familiar ground. But going on a few steps I came out on the edge of an unknown rocky cliff. I was now lost as well as blind.

During the hours I had wandered in reaching timberline I had had a vague feeling that I might be travelling in a circle, and might return to trees on the western slope of the Divide up which I had climbed. When I walked out on the edge of the cliff the feeling that I had doubled to the western slope became insistent. If true, this was most serious. To reach the nearest house on the west side of the range would be extremely difficult, even though I should discover just where I was. But I believed I was somewhere on the eastern slope.

I tried to figure out the course I had taken. Had I, in descending from the heights, gone too far to the right or to the left? Though fairly well acquainted with the country along this timberline, I was unable to recall a rocky cliff at this point. My staff found no bottom and warned me that I was at a jumping-off place.

Increasing coolness indicated that night was upon me. But darkness did not matter, my light had failed at noon. Going back along my trail a short distance I avoided the cliff and started on through the night down a rocky, forested, and snow-covered slope. I planned to get into the bottom of a cañon and follow downstream. Every few steps I shouted, hoping to attract the attention of a possible prospector, miner, or woodchopper. No voice answered. The many echoes, however, gave me an idea of the topography—of the mountain ridges and cañons before me. I listened intently after each shout and noticed the direction from which the reply came, its intensity, and the cross echoes, and concluded that I was going down into the head of a deep, forest-walled cañon, and, I hoped, travelling eastward.

Early engraving of Longs Peak, based on a William Henry Jackson photograph.

For points of the compass I appealed to the trees, hoping through my knowledge of woodcraft to orient myself. In the study of tree distribution I had learned that the altitude might often be approximated and the points of the compass determined by noting the characteristic kinds of trees.

Cañons of east and west trend in this locality carried mostly limber pines on the wall that faces south and mostly Engelmann spruces on the wall that faces the north. Believing that I was travelling eastward I turned to my right, climbed out of the cañon, and examined a number of trees along the slope. Most of these were Engelmann spruces. The slope probably faced north. Turning about I descended this slope and ascended the opposite one. The trees on this were mostly limber pines. Hurrah! Limber pines are abundant only on southern slopes. With limber pines on my left and Engelmann spruces on my right, I was now satisfied that I was travelling eastward and must be on the eastern side of the range.

To put a final check upon this—for a blind or lost man sometimes manages to do exactly the opposite of what he thinks he is doing—I examined lichen growths on the rocks and moss growths on the trees. In the deep cañon I dug down into the snow and examined the faces of low-lying boulders. With the greatest care I felt the lichen growth on the rocks. These verified the information that I had from the trees— but none too well. Then I felt over the moss growth, both long and short, on the trunks and lower limbs of trees, but this testimony was not absolutely convincing. The moss growth was so nearly even all the way around the trunk that I concluded that the surrounding topography must be such as to admit the light freely from all quarters, and also that the wall or slope on my right must be either a gentle one or else a low one and somewhat broken. I climbed to make sure. In a few minutes I was on a terrace—as I expected. Possibly back on the right lay a basin that might be tributary to this cañon. The reports made by the echoes of my shoutings said that this was true. A few minutes of travel down the cañon and I came to the expected incoming stream, which made its swift presence heard beneath its cover of ice and snow.

A short distance farther down the cañon I examined a number of trees that stood in thick growth on the lower part of what I thought was the southern slope. Here the character of the moss and lichens and their abundant growth on the northerly sides of the trees verified the testimony of the tree distribution and of previous moss and lichen growths. I was satisfied as to the points of the compass. I was on the eastern side of the Continental Divide travelling eastward.

After three or four hours of slow descending I reached the bottom. Steep walls rose on both right and left. The enormous rock masses and the entanglements of fallen and leaning trees made progress difficult. Feeling that if I continued in the bottom of the cañon I might come to a precipitous place down which I would be unable to descend, I tried to walk along one of the side walls, and thus keep above the bottom. But the walls were too steep and I got into trouble.

Out on a narrow, snow-corniced ledge I walked. The snow gave way beneath me and down I went over the ledge. As I struck, feet foremost, one snowshoe sank deeply. I wondered, as I wiggled out, if I had landed on another ledge. I had. Not desiring to have more tumbles, I tried to climb back up on the ledge from which I had fallen, but I could not do it. The ledge was broad and short and there appeared to be no safe way off. As I explored again my staff encountered the top of a dead tree that leaned against the ledge. Breaking a number of dead limbs off I threw them overboard. Listening as they struck the snow below I concluded that it could not be more than thirty feet to the bottom.

I let go my staff and dropped it after the limbs. Then, without taking off snowshoes, I let myself down the limbless trunk. I could hear water running beneath the ice and snow. I recovered my staff and resumed the journey.

In time the cañon widened a little and travelling became easier. I had just paused to give a shout when a rumbling and crashing high up the righthand slope told me that a snowslide was plunging down. Whether it would land in the cañon before me or behind me or on top of me could not be guessed. The awful smashing and crashing and roar proclaimed it of enormous size and indicated that trees and rocky débris were being swept onward with it. During the few seconds that I stood awaiting my fate, thought after thought raced through my brain as I recorded the ever-varying crashes and thunders of the wild, irresistible slide.

With terrific crash and roar the snowslide swept into the cañon a short distance in front of me. I was knocked down by the outrush or concussion of air and for several minutes was nearly smothered with the whirling, settling snow-dust and rock powder which fell thickly all around. The air cleared and I went on.

I had gone only a dozen steps when I came upon the enormous wreckage brought down by the slide. Snow, earthy matter, rocks, and splintered trees were flung in fierce confusion together. For three or four hundred feet this accumulation filled the cañon from wall to wall and was fifty or sixty feet high. The slide wreckage smashed the ice and dammed the stream. As I started to climb across this snowy débris a shattered place in the ice beneath gave way and dropped me into the water, but my long staff caught and by clinging to it I saved myself from going in above my hips. My snowshoes caught in the shattered ice and while I tried to get my feet free a mass of snow fell upon me and nearly broke my hold. Shaking off the snow I put forth all my strength and finally pulled my feet free of the ice and crawled out upon the débris. This was a close call and at last I was thoroughly, briefly, frightened.

As the wreckage was a mixture of broken trees, stones, and compacted snow I could not use my snowshoes, so I took them off to carry them till over the débris. Once across I planned to pause and build a fire to dry my icy clothes.

With difficulty I worked my way up and across. Much of the snow was compressed almost to ice by the force of contact, and in this icy cement many kinds of wreckage were set in wild disorder. While descending a steep place in this mass, carrying snowshoes under one arm, the footing gave way and I fell. I suffered no injury but lost one of the snowshoes. For an hour or longer I searched, without finding it.

The night was intensely cold and in the search my feet became almost frozen. In order to rub them I was about to take off my shoes when I came upon something warm. It proved to be a dead mountain sheep with one horn smashed off. As I sat with my feet beneath its warm carcass and my hands upon it, I thought how but a few minutes before the animal had been alive on the heights with all its ever wide-awake senses vigilant for its preservation; yet I, wandering blindly, had escaped with my life when the snowslide swept into the cañon. The night was calm, but of zero temperature or lower. It probably was crystal clear. As I sat warming my hands and feet on the proud master of the crags I imagined the bright, clear sky crowded thick with stars. I pictured to myself the dark slope down which the slide had come. It appeared to reach up close to the frosty stars.

But the lost snowshoe must be found, wallowing through the deep mountain snow with only one snowshoe would be almost hopeless. I had vainly searched the surface and lower wreckage projections but made one more search. This proved successful. The shoe had slid for a short distance, struck an obstacle, bounced upward over smashed logs, and lay about four feet above the general surface. A few moments more and I was beyond the snowslide wreckage. Again on snowshoes, staff in hand, I continued feeling my way down the mountain.

My ice-stiffened trousers and chilled limbs were not good travelling companions, and at the first cliff that I encountered I stopped to make a fire. I gathered two or three armfuls of dead limbs, with the aid of my hatchet, and soon had a lively blaze going. But the heat increased the pain in my eyes, so with clothes only partly dried, I went on. Repeatedly through the night I applied snow to my eyes trying to subdue the fiery torment.

From timberline I had travelled downward through a green forest mostly of Engelmann spruce with a scattering of fir and limber pine. I frequently felt of the tree trunks. But a short time after leaving my camp-fire I came to the edge of an extensive region that had been burned over. For more than an hour I travelled through dead standing trees, on many of which only the bark had been burned away; on others the fire had burned more deeply.

Pausing on the way down, I thrust my staff into the snow and leaned against a tree to hold snow against my burning eyes. While I was doing this two owls hooted happily to each other and I listened to their contented calls with satisfaction.

Hearing the pleasant, low call of a chickadee I listened. Apparently he was dreaming and talking in his sleep. The dream must have been a happy one, for every note was cheerful. Realizing that he probably was in an abandoned woodpecker nesting hole, I tapped on the dead tree against which I was leaning. This was followed by a chorus of lively, surprised chirpings, and one, two, three!—then several—chickadees flew out of a hole a few inches above my head. Sorry to have disturbed them I went on down the slope.

At last I felt the morning sun in my face. With increased light my eyes became extremely painful. For a time I relaxed upon the snow, finding it difficult to believe that I had been travelling all night in complete darkness. While lying here I caught the scent of smoke. There was no mistaking it. It was the smoke of burning aspen, a wood much burned in the cook-stoves of mountain people. Eagerly I rose to find it. I shouted again and again but there was no response. Under favourable conditions, keen nostrils may detect aspen-wood smoke for a distance of two or three miles.

The compensation of this accident was an intense stimulus to my imagination—perhaps our most useful intellectual faculty. My eyes, always keen and swift, had ever supplied me with almost an excess of information. But with them suddenly closed my imagination became the guiding faculty. I did creative thinking. With pleasure I restored the views and scenes of the morning before. Any one seeking to develop the imagination would find a little excursion afield, with eyes voluntarily blindfolded, a most telling experience.

Down the mountainside I went, hour after hour. My ears caught the chirp of birds and the fall of icicles which ordinarily I would hardly have heard. My nose was constantly and keenly analyzing the air. With touch and clasp I kept in contact with the trees. Again my nostrils picked up aspen smoke. This time it was much stronger. Perhaps I was near a house! But the whirling air currents gave me no clue as to the direction from which the smoke came, and only echoes responded to my call.

All my senses worked willingly in seeking wireless news to substitute for the eyes. My nose readily detected odours and smoke. My ears were more vigilant and more sensitive than usual. My fingers, too, were responsive from the instant that my eyes failed. Delightfully eager they were, as I felt the snow-buried trees, hoping with touch to discover possible trail blazes. My feet also were quickly, steadily alert to translate the topography.

Occasionally a cloud shadow passed over. In imagination I often pictured the appearance of these clouds against the blue sky and tried to estimate the size of each by the number of seconds its shadow took to drift across me.

Mid-afternoon, or later, my nose suddenly detected the odour of an ancient corral. This was a sign of civilization. A few minutes later my staff came in contact with the corner of a cabin. I shouted "Hello!" but heard no answer. I continued feeling until I came to the door and found that a board was nailed across it. The cabin was locked and deserted! I broke in the door.

In the cabin I found a stove and wood. As soon as I had a fire going I dropped snow upon the stove and steamed my painful eyes. After two hours or more of this steaming they became more comfortable. Two strenuous days and one toilsome night had made me extremely drowsy. Sitting down upon the floor near the stove I leaned against the wall and fell asleep. But the fire burned itself out. In the night I awoke nearly frozen and unable to rise. Fortunately, I had on my mittens, otherwise my fingers probably would have frozen. By rubbing my hands together, then rubbing my arms and legs, I finally managed to limber myself, and though unable to rise, I succeeded in starting a new fire. It was more than an hour before I ceased shivering; then, as the room began to warm, my legs came back to life and again I could walk.

I was hungry. This was my first thought of food since becoming blind. If there was anything to eat in the cabin, I failed to find it. Searching my pockets I found a dozen or more raisins and with these I broke my sixty-hour fast. Then I had another sleep, and it must have been near noon when I awakened. Again I steamed the eye pain into partial submission.

Going to the door I stood and listened. A camp-bird only a few feet away spoke gently and confidingly. Then a crested jay called impatiently. The camp-bird alighted on my shoulder. I tried to explain to the birds that there was nothing to eat. The prospector who had lived in this cabin evidently had been friendly with the bird neighbours. I wished that I might know him.

Again I could smell the smoke of aspen wood. Several shouts evoked echoes—nothing more. I stood listening and wondering whether to stay in the cabin or to venture forth and try to follow the snow-filled roadway that must lead down through the woods from the cabin. Wherever this open way led I could follow. But of course I must take care not to lose it.

In the nature of things I felt that I must be three or four miles to the south of the trail which I had planned to follow down the mountain. I wished I might see my long and crooked line of footmarks in the snow from the summit to timberline.

Hearing the open water in rapids close to the cabin, I went out to try for a drink. I advanced slowly, blind-man fashion, feeling the way with my long staff. As I neared the rapids, a water ouzel, which probably had lunched in the open water, sang with all his might. I stood still as he repeated his liquid, hopeful song. On the spot I shook off procrastination and decided to try to find a place where someone lived.

After writing a note explaining why I had smashed in the door and used so much wood, I readjusted my snowshoes and started down through the woods. I suppose it must have been late afternoon.

I found an open way that had been made into a road. The woods were thick and the open roadway readily guided me. Feeling and thrusting with my staff, I walked for some time at normal pace. Then I missed the way. I searched carefully, right, left, and before me for the utterly

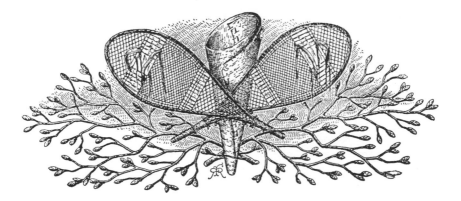

lost road. It had forked, and I had continued on the short stretch that came to an end in the woods by an abandoned prospect hole. As I approached close to this the snow caved in, nearly carrying me along with it. Confused by blinded eyes and the thought of oncoming night, perhaps, I had not used my wits. When at last I stopped to think I figured out the situation. Then I followed my snowshoe tracks back to the main road and turned into it.

For a short distance the road ran through dense woods. Several times I paused to touch the trees each side with my hands. When I emerged from the woods, the pungent aspen smoke said that I must at last be near a human habitation. In fear of passing it I stopped to use my ears. As I stood listening, a little girl gently, curiously, asked:

"Are you going to stay here to-night?"

NOTES

1. Grey, Zane, "An Appreciation of Grand Canyon," in John Kane, ed., *Picturesque America, Its Parks and Playgrounds* (New York: Resorts and Playgrounds of America, 1925), p. 125.

2. This chapter, p. 12,

3. Canby, Henry Seidel, *Walt Whitman: An American* (Boston: Houghton Mifflin, 1943), pp. 52-3.

4. DeVoto, Bernard, *The Year of Decision: 1846* (Boston: Houghton Mifflin, 1942), p. 37.

5. Boulding, Elise, *The Underside of History* (Boulder: Westview Press, 1976), p. 636.

6. Lord Birkenhead, *Rudyard Kipling* (New York: Random House, 1978), p. 91.

7. Burroughs, John, *Camping and Tramping with Roosevelt* (Boston: Houghton Mifflin, 1906), p. vii.

COMMENTS ON
THE SELECTIONS

INTRODUCTION. One must refer to narrative histories to appreciate the full scope of Colorado's history. Two of the most comprehensive and up-to-date histories are Carl Abbott, Stephen Leonard, and David McComb, *Colorado: A History of the Centennial State* (Boulder: Colorado Associated University Press, 1982) and Carl Ubbelohde, Maxine Benson, and Duane Smith, *A Colorado History* (Boulder: Pruett Publishing Co., 1982). Both books merit reading by any serious student of Colorado's past.

A few excellent first-hand accounts of frontier Colorado are still in print today. The most popular is probably Isabella Bird, *A Lady's Life in the Rocky Mountains* (Norman, Oklahoma: University of Oklahoma Press, 1969), originally published in 1888. A fascinating account of the Wet Mountain Valley by an eminent British naturalist is William A. Weber, ed., *Theodore D.A. Cockerell: Letters from West Cliff, Colorado, 1887-1889* (Boulder: Colorado Associated University Press, 1976); the book is valuable for both its human and natural history of the region. An anthology that contains fragments of a few first-hand accounts is Carl Ubbelohde, Maxine Benson, and Duane Smith, *A Colorado Reader* (Boulder: Pruett Publishing Co., 1982). More comprehensive than either *A Colorado Reader* or the present volume is W. Storrs Lee, ed., *Colorado: A Literary Chronicle* (New York: Grosset & Dunlap, 1970); though out of print, this book can probably be found in most Colorado libraries.

A few of the selections used in this volume have appeared in many different forms over the years. Others originated as periodical articles that later found their way into books; still others appeared but once in print before drifting into obscurity. In the case of the "classics"—particularly the Parkman, Twain, and Greeley chapters—I have foregone the usual practice of citing precise edition used, realizing that such information would be useless to those who did not have access to that particular edition. However, for the remainder of the selections complete bibliographic information has been provided.

FRANCIS PARKMAN (1846): *The Lonely Journey.* This selection is chapter 20 of *The Oregon Trail,* reproduced in its entirety. Parkman travelled West at a particularly propitious moment, the outbreak of the Mexican-American War. For a good overview of the West during this period, I recommend Bernard DeVoto's *1846: The Year of Decision* (Boston: Houghton Mifflin, 1942).

HORACE GREELEY (1859): *The Kansas Gold Diggings.* Dispatches 11 and 15 from *An Overland Journey* comprise this selection; the title is from chapter 11. Horace Greeley, of course, has special importance to Coloradans because a town in the northeastern part of the state was named for him, with his enthusiastic consent, by Nathan C. Meeker in 1869.

MARK TWAIN (1861): *Roughing It in Colorado.* The title of this selection is my own, not Twain's. The selection itself consists of the last paragraph of chapter VI as well as chapter VII of *Roughing It.* The letter to *The Denver Post* appeared separately many years later.

SAMUEL BOWLES (1868): *The Middle Park and an Indian Scare.* This selection consists of one complete and one abridged chapter from *The Switzerland of America* (Springfield, Mass.: S. Bowles, 1869): chapter V, "The Middle Park," pp. 65 79; and chapter IX, "An Indian Scare—The Twin Lakes," pp. 120–23 and pp. 127–30. From the latter chapter I have excised some of Bowles's moralizing about the "Indian problem."

HELEN HUNT JACKSON (1878): *Georgetown and the Terrible Mine.* From *Bits of Travel at Home* (Boston: Roberts, 1878), pp. 286–99.

WALT WHITMAN (1879): *Aerial Effects.* It is difficult to say precisely what Whitman intended to do with these random jottings. After his death they found their way into *Prose Works, Complete 1892* (Philadelphia: David McKay, 1897), pp. 142–50. We do know that the so-called interview with the Denver newspaper was actually a series of questions and answers that Whitman himself drew up, and later gave to the paper;

they had not been solicited. See Rollo Silver, "Walt Whitman Interviews Himself," *American Literature* 10 (March 1938): 84–7. Although the title of this chapter is of my own composition, the subheadings are all Whitman's.

EMILY FAITHFULL (1884): *Glimpses of Glory.* From *Three Visits to America* (New York: Fowler & Welles, 1884), chapter 10, pp. 133–38 and pp. 142–57. For a number of pages in Faithfull's chapter on Colorado in *Three Visits* she railed against the Irish agitator P. J. Sheridan, whose arrival in Denver was coincident with her own. Since her harangue had very little to do with her visit to Colorado, I have not included it in this selection.

RUDYARD KIPLING (1899): *The Man With Sorrow.* Rudyard Kipling's rambling narrative of his trip across America, *From Sea to Sea* (New York: Charles Scribners & Sons, 1899) was not neatly divided into chapters pertaining to his various stops along the way. Thus his Colorado escapades overlap chapters 33 and 34, pp. 214–26. "The Man With Sorrow" was the Baptist minister with whom Kipling traveled through Colorado.

THEODORE ROOSEVELT (1905): *A Colorado Bear Hunt.* This selection is from *Outdoor Pastimes of an American Hunter* (New York: Charles Scribners & Sons, 1908), chapter 2, pp. 68–99. In the same volume can be found Roosevelt's chronicle of pursuing mountain lion in Colorado, "With the Cougar Hounds." This essay is somewhat longer and more technical than the bear hunt story. For more on Roosevelt's Colorado adventures, on both wilderness and campaign trails, I recommend Agnes Wright Spring, "Theodore Roosevelt in Colorado," *The Colorado Magazine,* 35 (1958): 241–65.

ZANE GREY (1918): *Colorado Trails.* Chapter 2 from *Tales of Lonely Trails* (New York: Blue Ribbon Books, 1922), pp. 18–56.

ENOS MILLS (1920): *Snow-blinded on the Summit.* Chapter 1 of *The Adventures of a Nature Guide* (Boston: Houghton Mifflin Co., 1920), pp. 3–19.

PHOTO CREDITS

78 Georgetown from Crofutt's *Grip Sack Guide to Colorado.*

83 Mine shaft from *Crest of the Continent.*

88 Walt Whitman portrait from *Leaves of Grass* (Philadelphia: David McKay, 1900).

97 Spanish Peaks from *Crest of the Continent.*

102 Monument Park from *Crest of the Continent.*

108 Hall at Glen Eyrie courtesy of Western History Department, Denver Public Library.

113 Manitou from *Crest of the Continent.*

120 Rudyard Kipling portrait from *Plain Tales of the Hills* (New York: Charles Scribner's Sons, 1899).

125 Black Canyon from *Crest of the Continent.*

129 Curecanti Needle from *Crest of the Continent.*

132 Theodore Roosevelt portrait from *Outdoor Pastimes of an American Hunter* (New York: Charles Scribner's Sons, 1908).

136 Roosevelt and company leaving cabin from *Outdoor Pastimes of an American Hunter.*

143 Bear hunters from *Outdoor Pastimes of an American Hunter.*

148 Roosevelt and bear from *Outdoor Pastimes of an American Hunter.*

158 Zane Grey portrait from *Tales of Lonely Trails* (New York: Blue Ribbon Books, 1922).

163 Trapper's Lake courtesy of Western History Department, Denver Public Library.

168 Elk from *Crofutt's Grip Sack Guide to Colorado.*

179 Grizzly Bears courtesy of Rocky Mountain National Park Historical Collections.

192 Enos Mills portrait courtesy of Rocky Mountain National Park Historical Collections.

197 Longs Peak from *Crofutt's Grip Sack Guide to Colorado.*